Praise for *Rescued: Saving Animals f*

"Compelling, fascinating, and — most important

— Ben Stein, author, &

"A must-read that I couldn't put down, *Rescued* wil.

— Marc Bekoff, professor of biology at the University of Colorado
and editor of the *Encyclopedia of Animal Behavior*

"*Rescued* serves as a reminder that saving animals' precious lives is not only noble but also a moral imperative."

— Gretchen Wyler, vice president of the Humane Society of the United States (Hollywood Office) and retired executive producer of Genesis Awards

"This book offers vital, in-the-trenches information for saving animals' lives...Read it and reap!"

— Dr. Marty Becker, resident veterinarian on *Good Morning America* and author of *The Healing Power of Pets*

"Hurricane Katrina taught us that public policy must be revised to reflect the love between people and their nonhuman family members. *Rescued* is a finely written, touching, and important book that will warm the hearts of all readers whose animals are an indispensable part of the family."

— Karen Dawn, founder of the animal advocacy media watch DawnWatch.com

Praise for *Angel Dogs*

"Reading *Angel Dogs: Divine Messengers of Comfort* is like taking a walk in the park on a sunny day with your favorite dog. This wonderful collection of stories will bring back memories of the sweet, delightful, and touching times you have spent with your own loyal canine friends."

— from the foreword by Willard Scott of NBC's *Today Show*

"The Andersons have done it again! *Angel Dogs* is a healing and heart-opening book. Highly recommended."

— Doreen Virtue, PhD, author of *Angel Medicine* and *Healing with the Angels*

Praise for *Angel Cats*

"Angels come to us in many ways. Some are never identified, and some come to us and we don't even know they changed our lives, maybe even saved us, until there is a realization. This book is enlightening and will make you take many a close look at your 'angel.' "

— Tippi Hedren, actress and animal activist

"As a believer and one who lives the message, my heart was touched by *Angel Cats*. I have long realized that it is not an accident that three-quarters of our *lifeline* is *feline*. So read, laugh, cry, and become a more complete human being through the angel cats and the lifeline they provide."

— Dr. Bernie S. Siegel, author of *365 Prescriptions for the Soul* and *Love, Medicine & Miracles*

Praise for *Rainbows and Bridges: An Animal Companion Memorial Kit*

"If you are facing or have faced the loss of a beloved animal friend, let this kit be your companion and your comfort. There exists no better exploration of this landscape of loss than you will find here."

— Susan Chernak McElroy, author of *Animals as Teachers & Healers* and *All My Relations*

Praise for *God's Messengers*

"To speak of 'lower' animals is both arrogant and blasphemous. All traditional peoples have viewed animals as messengers and mediators of the divine, which is a lesson we need to relearn. *God's Messengers* is a bold reminder that consciousness takes many forms and is not restricted to humans."

— Larry Dossey, MD, author of *Healing Beyond the Body* and *Healing Words*

"As a lifelong animal lover, I am delighted to see them celebrated in such a positive way. You and your pet will enjoy reading this together."

— Betty White, author and actress

ANGEL
horses

Also by Allen and Linda Anderson

Angel Animals: Exploring Our Spiritual Connection with Animals

Angel Cats: Divine Messengers of Comfort

Angel Dogs: Divine Messengers of Love

God's Messengers: What Animals Teach Us about the Divine

Rainbows and Bridges: An Animal Companion Memorial Kit

Rescued: Saving Animals from Disaster

ANGEL
horses

Divine Messengers
of Hope

Allen & Linda Anderson

NEW WORLD LIBRARY
NOVATO, CALIFORNIA

New World Library
14 Pamaron Way
Novato, California 94949

Page 27, "The New Animal Alchemy," from *The Language of Miracles: A Celebrated Psychic Teaches You to Talk to Animals*, by Amelia Kinkade, copyright © 2006. Reprinted with permission of New World Library. All rights reserved.

Page 153, "Fashion," from *All My Relations: Living with Animals as Teachers and Healers*, by Susan Chernak McElroy, copyright © 2004. Reprinted with permission of New World Library. All rights reserved.

Photographs on back cover and pages xix, 69, 119, 161, and 210 © 2006 Lois Stanfield/LightSource Images (www.lightsource-images.com). Used with permission. All rights reserved.

Text design and typography by Tona Pearce Myers

ISBN-13: 978-1-57731-518-6
Printed in the U.S.A.

New World Library is a proud member of the Green Press Initiative.

Distributed by Publishers Group West

Contents

Chapter Three
Courage and Endurance

Chapter Four
Spiritual Connection and the Afterlife

Introduction

*H*orse surveys his pasture, a kingdom inhabited by verdant grass, bales of hay, and fellow equines who graze and mill as if dancing a slow waltz.

Human approaches. A female, small in size, walking confidently on two legs, smelling like a predator. She has so far been a friend, not an enemy, so there is no reason to bolt and run. With gentle hands, making soft-voice sounds, she strokes horse skin, so sensitive that a fly's feet can tingle nerve endings throughout the entire body.

Horse knows of Human ways and tolerates when she places heaviness on his body and inside his mouth. He hears her words commanding him and feels the sensation of her flesh touching his.

He does not understand her language, only her thoughts, slightest movements, and feelings.

Human says, "Carry me into the wind. Take me to the places where I can glide close to high tree branches. I will use your body to reach the sky. Your scenting will guide me to where the sun sets. Your eyes will see to escape danger. Your lungs will expand with breath to endure the miles. Your heart will remind me to seek what I have lost. Your spirit will listen to the voices I do not hear. You are Horse. I will care for you. Together, we will journey."

Horse nods his head and snorts. He is not convinced.

He bends down and mouths her hand, looking for the stray gift of sweetness hiding there. Finding it, he scrapes his big lips against her palm, gathers it to his wide teeth, and nibbles. He munches, considering her proposal.

Human croons to Horse. She sings of hooves drumming the ground, of meadows filled with fresh clover patches and spring flowers, of cold and gurgling streams, of breezes whipping through his mane and cooling his straining body. She sings of love, friendship, and protection that only a kind Human can offer to the herd.

Horse nickers softly. He places his head on Human's shoulder, his long neck encircling her short one. He smells the familiar fragrance of her hair as his chest presses against her heart. Horse accepts the deal.

History and Horse

As it turns out, Horse initiated the deal between Horse and Human.

In 1867 archeologists found on the American continent the remains of the Dawn Horse, which dated back sixty million years, to the Eocene period. The species called Eohippus evolved about a million years ago into *Equus caballus*, ancient ancestor to the modern horse. Migrating from the American continent by using land bridges to Europe and Asia, Equus and its many species made their way into every corner of the world and adapted to every climate on the planet. About ten thousand years ago horses went extinct in the Americas. As horses vanished from the western part of the world, Middle Eastern desert people raced them. Mongolians rode them into battle. African jungles gave them stripes and turned them into zebras. Europeans hitched them to carriages and rode them everywhere.

Horses returned to the Americas when Spanish conquistadors brought them back to what was actually the horse's original home. Native Americans fell in love with Equus, domesticating horses for transportation and to hunt for food.[1] Paul Revere rode a borrowed, unnamed horse to Lexington to warn rebellious Americans that British troops were coming to attack their city.[2] Foreign settlers could not have conquered the new lands of America without horses to drive their wagons westward, pull their plows across plains and farmlands, and deliver their mail by Pony Express.

Horses carry history on their backs.

Today, 4 percent of American households have a horse, with 3 percent boarding their horses at home and 1 percent stabling them elsewhere.[3] There are approximately 9.2 million horses in the United States: 40 percent of them provide recreational activities for people; 30 percent are kept as show horses; 12 percent run in races.[4] The Minnesota Horse Expo, one of the largest horse fairs in the country and one that has taken place for twenty-four years, draws fifty breeds of horses together for a three-day, event-filled weekend with

55,000 people milling about the state fairgrounds. The horse industry in this state alone provides an economic impact of $32 billion.[5] To say that the horse industry is big business in this country would be an understatement. Even as key actors in movies, horses are income-producing stars.

Getting to Know Horses

When we were children, we rode horses on well-worn trails with our schoolmates but never became especially proficient. We had the obligatory photos taken of child wearing cowboy hat and sitting astride horse. As adults, we occasionally go horseback riding. We haven't had many close encounters with horses recently, although our fascination with their speed, ability, and beauty has continued to grow over the years.

Linda recalls, like many children of her generation, repeatedly reading Anna Sewell's classic novel, *Black Beauty*. "After each time I read the book," she says, "my mother would ask, 'Why are you crying? You knew how it would end.' I had to agree with her logic, but

Linda hugging a horse

something in that story of the forlorn little horse moved me in an abiding way. I would put it aside for a month or so and then read it again — always with fresh tears over its poignancy."

Allen's childhood experiences with horses came to fruition in his early teens. He says that going to a local stable to ride the trails offered one of the best escapes from the pressures of adolescence. While the horses were used to having amateurs ride them on the designated trails, the connection he felt one afternoon with a horse named Brownie was powerful and healing.

Brownie was an older mare who appeared to take her duties one step past her job description. Doing her work for years, she knew the trails by heart — the locations of low branches, the holes, turns, and smaller, more interesting paths off the main passageway. One day Brownie gave Allen a tour of her world. He describes the afternoon by saying, "We went everywhere. Brownie was in charge, and I felt safe. For the first time in months, I was living in the moment, not constantly thinking, and she was helping me to relax by letting my concerns and stress slip away."

Safety was Brownie's motto. She would gallop around low branches, take a less-traveled side path, slow down at just the right time so Allen could have the opportunity to become aware of his surroundings, viewing the small grazing field and an almost invisible stream slowly trickling through the pebbles. Normally, as a young boy, he would have ignored the beauty surrounding him

Allen visiting with Zeke

because he was in an anxious state of mind. He says, "I have no doubt that Brownie wanted to show this child, who was quickly becoming a man, what was in her world. Hers was a different world from mine because it veered off the main fast track. I look back and realize the sweet brown mare, through her actions that day, helped me to slow down and not rush to take on more in life."

When our editor at New World Library, Georgia Hughes, asked us to write about horses as the next book in our Divine Messengers/Angel Animals series, we were a bit apprehensive because we don't have a horse in our lives now.

We do, however, appreciate the deeply spiritual relationships between souls wearing human bodies and souls clothed in fur, feathers, and fins. Since doing hands-on research with horses and assembling the wonderful anthology of stories for this book, we are even more impressed with how innately spiritual the human-horse relationship can be. These stories show horses rising far above the instincts of their species and listening to the inner call of the Divine. Time and again, they serve as angelic messengers when humans are under duress. If people can still the chattering of minds and ignore social, intellectual, and cultural restrictions about exactly what is and is not possible, horses speak to them with astonishing clarity.

Horses are sensitive to everything and everyone around them. This makes them both receptors and messengers for God, Divine Spirit, the Sacred, or whatever you want to call the love that flows through all creation. Perhaps because they are prey animals, horses have had to learn how to tune in to the slightest changes in their inner worlds and outer environments. We learned by writing this book that if you are ever in doubt about the direction to take in your life and you need a second opinion, you couldn't do better than to listen to a horse's advice.

This is why we sought the help of our dear friend Lois Stanfield and her wise horse, Zeke. We first met Zeke when Lois wrote about her spiritual relationship with him for our book *God's Messengers: What Animals Teach Us about the Divine* (New World Library, 2003). Be sure to read Lois's wonderful journey-of-a-lifetime story about Zeke in chapter 1 of this book.

Whenever we went out with Lois to visit Zeke in his stable, he was always the most gracious host. He agreed to have his photo taken with us for this book. And he extended his generosity by letting us create an advice column for him to author.

"Ask Zeke" appears at the end of each chapter. We posed questions to Zeke that many people wonder about and then answered them, to the best of our ability, with what we thought he wanted to say.

Lois assures us that Zeke has lots of opinions and is quite talkative. We don't bill ourselves as animal communicators, but by gazing into a photo that shows Zeke's soulful eyes staring back at us, we tried to tune in to this beautiful soul. Words flowed onto the

Allen and Linda with Zeke (© 2006 by Lois Stanfield/LightSource Images)

page that went far beyond anything we would have thought to say. You'll have to decide for yourself if Zeke allowed us to respectfully tap into the horse consciousness for answers to some of life's most perplexing questions.

Getting to Know Horse People

We observed that most horse people are straightforward, decisive, and somewhat fearless. Making commitments to care for animals who might live as long as fifty years and become equine lawn mowers instead of riding companions as they age requires people who keep their promises no matter what and are proud of it.

We also noticed that there seem to be two kinds of horse people — ones who get it and ones who don't. By *it*, we mean understanding and respecting horses as sentient, conscious spiritual beings. The ones who don't accept the higher nature, intelligence, and spirit of the horse often operate by dominance, control, and a sort of macho posturing designed to intimidate both horses and people. Of course, we are making generalizations here. Each species is complex, and individuals can't be glibly categorized or labeled. But you get the picture. You know the types.

Consequently, it appeared to us that before revealing themselves, horses always check out whether they're dealing with a horse person who gets it or one who does not. Horses wear blank expressions or masks of quiet wariness. A horse quickly learns the art of discretion. Humans are capricious at best and cruel at worst. There is not much the horse can do about it either way.

So horses have perfected passive-aggressiveness to assert their individuality and covertly express their opinions. Horses make jokes at humans' expense — playfully if the person is nice and secretly if the human is mean. To be themselves, spooked or stubborn horses rise up on powerful haunches and toss their human riders. They bite and kick when threatened or guarding their turf. Horses escape by using whatever resources they can muster to unlock paddock or stall gates with their teeth or kick down doors. Freeing themselves of human burdens becomes a mission for those who long to run freely and feel the blood of wild animals coursing through their veins.

Fortunately for readers of this book and for us, bona fide horse people who get it were willing to share their stories. They honor and respect horses and here provide glimpses of the experiences and relationships that are possible between spiritual beings who view one another as equals.

Terminology

Can a person own a horse?

Horses are bought and sold as commodities. This is not the same as owning them. Horses can be beaten down physically and emotionally. This also is not the same as owning them. We have concluded that it is impossible to own a horse — or any other animal, for that matter.

This said, many of the contributing authors in this book use the word *owner* because ownership is how people move horses from one place to another. After speaking and corresponding with our contributing authors many times, we believe that they would agree that the spirit, the heart, of a horse is too great to be possessed just because money has been exchanged. So for purposes of smoother communication, we have left the word *owner* in their stories. Trying to substitute preferable words like *guardian* or *caretaker* or the *horse's person* seemed to complicate and slow down the storytelling. The truth of the matter is that in today's society, owning horses is how the law protects human-horse relationships.

We have continued, though, as we do in all our writings, to refer to horses as *who, she, he, they* and not as *it* or *that*. This terminology may seem like a small distinction, but with the preciseness of language, it proclaims that horses are not objects.

For other terms that horse people understand but that sound like a foreign language to the general public, we rely on the context of the sentences or stories for definition. It slows momentum too much to stop and define dressage, show horse, or training terms. Readers who are interested in understanding more will no doubt do some additional research.

However, a few terms used frequently in the book need explanation. One of them is the practice of describing a horse's size in *hands*. Horses used to be measured by starting from the ground and placing the palm of your hand vertically against the horse while pointing your fingers at the tail and moving your hands up to the horse's shoulders, or withers. A hand was estimated to be about four inches. So to find a horse's size in feet and inches, multiply the hands figure by four inches and then divide that number by twelve inches. Basically, a 17-hand horse is as huge as a young elephant. A pony would be smaller than 14 hands.

When someone says that a horse nickers, this is a sign of friendliness. Neighing is the equivalent of a loud hello or the question, Where are you?

Some authors in the book refer to training their horses with *natural horsemanship* methods. According to the Naturally Penzance website article "What Is Natural Horsemanship?" the system is "the art of working, training, riding with horses in a manner which works with the horse's behavior, instincts, and personality in an easy and kind manner." (Sounds good to us!) World-renowned trainers such as John Lyons, Pat Parelli, Buck Brannaman, Tom Dorrance, Linda Tellington-Jones, Clinton Anderson, and Monty Roberts, among others, all have their own styles and practices of natural horsemanship that they teach to thousands of horse owners annually.[6]

While doing research for this book, we met a delightful woman who practices natural horsemanship with a small herd of rescued horses. Suzanne Perry and her husband and two children are all horse lovers. Suzanne likes to tell the story about her mother driving to work one day watching in shock as her five-year-old daughter took an unsupervised, bareback, full-gallop ride on a neighbor's horse while clutching the horse's streaming mane in the wind and laughing and crying for joy. In Suzanne's world there are only two types of people — those who love horses and those who don't. She refers to herself as an *animal sensitive* who instinctively anticipates horses' needs and has great success educating young riders. She says that to her "horse manure is the perfume of the gods." She calls herself "a two-legged horse" and "an interpreter for the equine mind."

Suzanne graciously let us follow her and her daughter, "who rides a horse so well that she looks like she has Velcro on her bottom." They introduced us to the horses whom Suzanne says nobody else wants. With camera ready and pad and paper in hand, we interviewed Suzanne, her children,

Linda taking notes while interviewing Suzanne's horse

and her horses. They gave us thorough lessons about today's horse world. When we left the barn and pastures where Suzanne works, she said something very profound, a theme that is reflected throughout this book. Suzanne said, "I'm seeing me through my horse's eyes."

Join Us for a Journey into Angel Horse World

The subtitle of *Angel Horses* is *Divine Messengers of Hope*. This book is divided into four chapters, each of which contains stories that chronicle experiences people have had with horses who gave them hope. With their innate wisdom and sixty-million-year-old world-view, horses offer hope for love and the fulfillment of dreams, hope for having courage and endurance, hope for healing and regaining health, and hope for spiritual connection and reuniting after death.

The people who contributed their stories wrote short biographies about themselves. Be sure to read them in the back of the book. You will find that these contributors are ordinary people who have gained spiritual insights because of their relationships with a horse or horses.

If you open your heart and mind to them, these stories will remind you of your own glimpses into invisible realms. The stories will fill you with love and gratitude. They will introduce or reacquaint you with the spirit of the horse. These stories of angels among us will give you hope.

ANGEL
horses

CHAPTER ONE

Love and Dreams

Now, the wild white horses play,
Champ and chafe and toss in the spray.

— Matthew Arnold

Each year three to four hundred captured wild horses are shipped to the Hutchinson Correctional Facility in Wichita, Kansas, to become part of the Kansas Wild Horse Program. At the prison the inmates gentle the horses and prepare them to be adopted into homes. The horses learn to load into and unload from trailers. They learn to climb up hills and calmly back down and to step over and around obstacles. According to "Paroled Horse: The Kansas Wild Horse Program Gives Inmates and Mustangs a Second Chance" by Denise Parsons, "An inmate must achieve the highest level of good behavior and trust by the warden before being allowed to take part in the program."

The training program provides inmates with the opportunity to have responsibility for another being and to feel pride in their accomplishments. The men have to qualify for the program and be minimum security risks. They ride the horses at Sand Hills State Park, not at the prison. Neither horses nor prisoners have ever tried to escape.[1]

This program uses prisoners as trainers and companions for animals who need a friend. Its success gives hope to the inmates and to the horses because the power of love and friendship opens up a world of freedom for all of them.

As herd animals, horses form natural friendships with other horses and with humans who become like their herd. When pastured together, horses pair off with compatible horses. Claire Albinson writes in the book *In Harmony with Your Horse: How to Build a Lasting Relationship*, "During the ritual of mutual grooming, the heartbeat of both horses will drop as they become more relaxed. Horses will eventually mutually groom with all the members of their group, thus reinforcing the bond between the whole group... These friendships are very important to the horses, and they will display a strong desire to be reunited with their 'friend,' if they are separated, by calling loudly and by showing agitation."[2]

Because horses don't live inside homes with people and curl up on their laps like cats, the relationships between humans and horses are unlike those with any other domesticated animal. Horses must be loved at a distance until they let you into their hearts with the acknowledgment that you are a nice person after all, maybe even a friend.

Humans experience unique forms of companionship with horses. A rider's skin touches a horse's skin, feeling the ripple of muscle, hearing for hours at a time the symphony of breaths, snorts, whinnies, and hooves striking the ground. The pungent scent of horse sweat and the sight of a mane whipping in the wind like a flag add to the sensory delight of the bonding between horse and human. The memory of ancient times and past pacts provides visceral, sensual interactions that humans have with no other creatures on this earth.

This chapter illustrates the hope that horses bring for finding love and the part they play in making dreams come true. It shows that love arrives disguised in many forms and through a variety of experiences.

Listen, now, as the love songs that horses and people sing to each other bring hope and divine messages.

Emily's Song

Kevin Schwaderer
Edon, Ohio

*T*he teachers at our small school knew little about Emily. She seemed to be another forgotten foster child enrolled in our special-needs school in central Ohio. Her birth parents had come to our town at some time in the past. After some legal issues, Emily and her younger brother had been made wards of the court and placed with foster parents. The birth parents had promptly disappeared, seemingly into thin air.

When I met Emily she was a thin, withdrawn eight-year-old with a pale complexion and stringy blond hair. Her posture and demeanor spoke of much abuse and neglect. She couldn't allow anyone to be close to her and would seek out the farthest point in any room, away from other people. Emily never spoke, and other children left her alone. Her eyes conveyed that social isolation was just fine with her.

Emily's only companion was a small stuffed pony of threadbare plaid fabric, which had seen many better years. She treated it not so much as a toy but as her contemporary, holding in-depth, telepathic conversations with the toy pony for hours on end. Its straggly mane and empty spots where button eyes should have been made it a perfect candidate for either extensive repairs or a replacement, but

Emily would have none of that. Several people tried to take the stuffed pony from Emily long enough to either clean or refurbish it, but she greeted these efforts with wails of anguish. Her moments of separation from the stuffed pony so upset her that it would take the rest of the day for Emily's sobbing to be relieved.

Social workers and psychologists worked with Emily for many weeks, trying to determine the exact course that they should take to help her. Emily's younger brother acted ostensibly normal. His characteristic good attitude presented a stark contrast to Emily's reclusive and closed life.

"Autism," said one knowledgeable professional.

"Withdrawal or anxiety syndrome, at the very least," said another.

Whatever her diagnosis, Emily's symptoms told us that her world was not a pretty one.

Such was her life until the day of the farm trip.

That day the plan was to take Emily's class to the Valley Farm for the afternoon. Our numbers totaled twenty-one children, all with varying forms of special needs. The children were excited at having a day off from regular school, basking in the bright fall sun, enjoying a picnic and a trip in the bus.

The bus ride to the farm was uneventful. Teachers and their aides busily scooted about, checking up on their charges. Most of the children took catnaps, as the drone of the bus almost immediately lulled them to sleep. Emily, as usual, had positioned herself as far away from others as possible. She sat in the left rear corner of that long, yellow bus with, of course, her only companion, the unnamed stuffed pony.

In the late eighties, most people didn't give a lot of thought to the physically challenged, and most buildings and homes made no specific accommodations. The farm we were visiting was ahead of its time. It had ramps, slides, and several special sets of stairs for adults or children with poor motor skills. It even had properly equipped restrooms.

The farm's animals were kept in a large, open setting that allowed visitors to intermingle easily with them. There were goats, puppies, and kittens in abundance and even a variety of small, sweet-natured piglets. Throw in a very tame milk cow, and we had all that a trip to the farm should be. Except at this farm, there were also the horses. And what an attraction to the children they were!

Two older, stabled quarter horses provided rides or lessons for children who could ride. For those who could not ride, there were the ponies. Three Shetlands — two mares and one gelding — stood together in the back corner of a paddock and patiently watched as this motley group made its way toward them. The mares, more gregarious, clustered next to the fence when the children drew near. They made it clear that they were more than willing to trade their affection for any bit of treat that we might offer.

The old gelding timidly held back. When I asked about the gelding, the farm operators told me that this horse was new there and probably wouldn't ever be well suited for children because of his skittish nature.

The operators said that the gelding had originally been a child's pony. When the child outgrew the pony after a few years, he languished in a field, alone and forgotten, without regular food, care, or shelter.

The gelding had since been rescued and brought to the farm.

While his physical health was now good, his emotional state was not. His inability to trust was expected to keep him from ever being all that he could be. Whenever children came to visit, the operators of the farm separated him from the tiny herd and isolated him inside the barn so that children could safely get into the area with the other ponies.

Everyone had a wonderful time that sunny fall afternoon. As the day grew short, it soon became time to do what we all dreaded — head back into town. We packed baskets, emptied coolers, and loaded children and wheelchairs onto the bus one by one.

Then we realized that we couldn't find Emily anywhere. We looked through all the barns and buildings. We searched the paddocks and lots. The little eight-year-old seemed nowhere to be found. We were frantic.

I decided to retrace our steps. I trudged back through the buildings and barns. As I reached the open barn door, I heard something that lightly touched the edge of my senses. I stood at the door, trying to identify it. A couple of romping kittens in mock battle on top of a stack of hay drew my attention, but I knew this wasn't what I had heard. Listening closely, I heard the sound again and finally realized it was someone singing. Very low and very soft, but nevertheless, this was distinctly singing.

I moved quietly toward the sound. As I turned the corner, there in a stall, standing quietly munching hay, was the little gelding who couldn't trust. At his feet, lying flat on the ground and looking up at the horse with wide and adoring eyes, was our missing Emily.

Shivers swept over me at the ethereal sound of her voice. I stood in awe for a moment, taking in the gift before me. On the fresh hay, with sunlight streaming in, this frail, fair girl, who had never uttered a single word or sound around us, sang softly, melodiously, and earnestly to this wise old gelding. He stood there, scant inches away from Emily's face. His eyes looked deep into hers, locked in what seemed to be a trance, as Emily continued her song for him. The more she sang, the louder she became, until her beautiful voice could be heard throughout that old barn. It was as if all else in the world had fallen silent except for that beautiful songbird crooning to that old, graying muzzle.

Kevin with another special friend, Mona

Entranced, I didn't hear anyone come up behind me. I finally turned and found nearly a half dozen others who were as mesmerized by that song as I. Emily's classroom teacher was so enthralled that tears were streaming down her face.

It was then that the pair noticed they were not alone, and the sound died off slowly. Emily sat up. For a moment I thought she might run and hide. Instead, she looked at me and said simply, "I'm sorry."

I asked, "Whatever for?"

She didn't answer but looked back at that old bay gelding, sighed, crossed beside him, and reached out to draw his neck into her grasp. I swear that he hooked his head over her shoulder and managed to hug her back.

Emily gazed into his eyes and ever so softly said something that only he could hear. I noticed that she had left her ragged, stuffed plaid pony sitting on the gelding's stall board. As I went to retrieve it, Emily said, "No, I told him I'd leave it for him. He needs a friend. He's all alone. He needs it more than I do." Her voice was strangely powerful, and a golden glow emanated from her.

We all were thunderstruck at her generosity. In those few minutes together, the abandoned child and abused horse had seemed to fuse into one. She drew strength from him, and he received compassion from her.

Emily quietly followed us back to the buses. We finished our tasks and loaded up to leave, thankful that things had turned out as they did. I knew we had witnessed a miracle.

On the ride to school, Emily remained her quiet self. But her foster parents called her teacher the next morning and said that at the dinner table the prior evening Emily had asked for something. The request stunned them because this child had not spoken in all the months she had lived with them. Emily had asked them if she could go back to the farm sometime soon.

Emily, indeed, went back to that farm many times.

Although Emily could never be considered a rowdy child, she became vocal and adjusted well to life with her foster parents. They eventually adopted her and gave her the life she had always dreamed of having.

I don't know what happened to Emily years later. I don't know what happened with that wise old gelding who had trust issues. I lost touch with everyone else who had been there that amazing day. But sometimes I wonder if Emily is somewhere singing for her own pony, and I hope she is doing well. Perhaps, all these years later, she even has a little Emily of her own.

I did speak to the operators of that farm not long after our visit. They told me the name of the wise, old gelding who had coaxed a song from Emily. It was, of all things, Angelo.

Meditation

When have you met a horse who responded to your song?

The Artist Is a Horse

Renée Chambers
Reno, Nevada

*T*here he is, in all his glory, standing at his easel, stroking the watercolor paper with deliberate and precise strokes. His passion is evident, and the art is captivating. As he paints with pride and fulfillment in the green pasture, his creation comes to life. It all makes perfect sense, except this artist is a horse.

His name is Cholla, a magnificent 1,300-pound abstract expressionist, standing 15.2 hands. The son of a mustang stallion and quarter horse mare, Cholla is a wonderful combination, in my opinion, although I am no authority. His coloring is copper buckskin highlighted with black mane and tail, a black dorsal stripe, and zebralike markings on his legs. His face is that of an angel.

As Cholla paints, he masterfully rolls a delicate artist's brush held in his teeth and executes his desired, willful strokes. Next he flicks the brush and splashes paint on the canvas with graceful intent. He turns his head and gives the brush to me, his loving assistant. I smile and apply more paint to the bristles. Cholla gently takes the brush from my hand and returns with conviction to his creation. The artist is at work.

In this green, lush pasture his palomino buddy watches intently from the other side of the fence. Cholla's decision to paint overrides his desire for food or herding with one of his own species. The scene appears somewhat unnatural, yet it feels perfectly natural. It's a stimulating sensation to watch him paint, and the energy is pure. There is no denying that Cholla positively loves to paint. His intelligence is as evident as his uninterrupted focus.

Cholla watched me paint fences for years. That's as far as my talents go in the world of paint; my artistry lies in the dance.

One day as I painted Cholla's corral, with my equine companion following close behind, my husband, Robert, shouted, "Why don't you get that horse to help you?"

I giggled and continued, with Cholla still in pursuit. I was about halfway done with this chore and was thinking I'd rather be in my flower garden. (I can grow anything, so I always say that mine is a *fluorescent neon* green thumb.) I adore flowers and had recently taken a six-week adult watercolor class devoted to painting flowers. I was pretty pathetic in the class, but it had still been fun to try.

Inspired by the class, I had purchased high-end watercolor paints complete with quality brushes and stacks of expensive watercolor paper. After the class session was over, I placed the pristine supplies on the top shelf of my guest room closet. Little did I know they would become dear objects to my horse.

As I trudged along the corral fence line that day, Cholla stayed with me. I could tell he wanted to help. His curiosity and interest were overwhelmingly peculiar. He focused on what I was doing to the point that nothing could distract him from watching me. He has always loved to hold things in his mouth, ever since I got him when he was five, but there was no way I was going to let him have that big, drippy brush full of white latex paint. I continued working while Cholla remained well behaved and didn't delay my progress.

While I painted, I thought back to when I first got Cholla. He was volatile, since he had been broke the old-fashioned way, with ropes and force, a method called sacking out. To do this, the cowboys halter the horse, tie ropes to each limb, get the horse to the ground, and tie him off so he is fully restrained. The horse fights until he is completely traumatized and exhausted. Cholla, now twenty years old, still carries deep scars on his hind legs, at the fetlocks, from these ropes. At the horse's point of greatest exhaustion, the cowboys rub ten-pound sacks of flour up and down the horse's body. This is supposed to teach the horse that humans are more powerful.

Sacking out works to destroy the spirits of many horses, but all it did for Cholla was teach him not to trust humans and their ropes. Cholla's spirit and intelligence were not diminished from this cruel practice. If anything, they were heightened. His intelligence was much greater than their exhausting attempt to manipulate his mind.

Cholla is the only horse I have ever owned, and I have spent years gaining his trust. To this day, if he feels threatened he will let me know it. Over the years he has mellowed somewhat, but his spirit is grand and invincible. I respect and love him in the deepest way because I have learned many lessons from him. He has taught me to stay calm even in challenging situations. If I stay calm, so does he, and my world stays calm.

Thinking of Cholla's unbroken spirit and great heart, I continued my tedious chore of slopping paint on the corral boards. My wannabe apprentice was still paying close attention to what I was doing. Then, the light went on: *Hey, I have all those expensive supplies I bought for the art class. I bet Cholla would love to use them and*

*paint. I know some elephants paint — why not Cholla? He's as intelli-
gent and certainly has a memory like an elephant.*

The next day I tacked a piece of paper to the fence and showed
Cholla how to make one stroke. That was all it took. Cholla understood the concept of painting from the very beginning. I held out
the brush to him, and he gently took it in his teeth. He didn't try to
break or eat the brush but turned his head and went right to the
paper. It took him a few times to calculate the distance between his
brush and the paper, but he quickly rose to the challenge. From the
start, he used gentle strokes.

The first painting that Cholla did was abstract, but in it I found
many spiritual images that represent my life and are quite private
and intimate to me. This is, of course, my own interpretation of the
art, but I get very emotional when I gaze at his first piece. The second piece, which he created moments later, is a self-portrait I titled
Zen — Self-Portrait. It consists of two eyes, a mouth, a jaw line, and
forelocks. The image is not only of a horse but is undeniably that of
Cholla himself.

Cholla's demeanor was elegant and peaceful upon completing
these first two pieces. He was not boisterous or precocious about
his accomplishment, and he had obviously enjoyed himself. I was
amazed and thrilled.

The next day I purchased a big, sturdy, ornate easel made of iron
with fancy scrolls at the top. It was a tripod device with a chain sup-
porting the back leg. A couple of days later I set up the easel in the
pasture, and Cholla made the transition to it without hesitation. His
strokes became even more fluid since the easel offered additional
space for him to create. He used many vertical strokes on his first
easel paintings but soon developed an engaging and charming style

of his own. No one moves the paper or easel, but I have to put the paint on his brush for him. After all, he is a horse, still quite wild and with a mind of his own.

When Cholla paints, he is not in any way egotistical or cocky. He is sweet as can be. Now painting is a regular part of his life. He paints many birds. Anyone can see the birds in his paintings. Also, he paints horses. People in the art world have told me that Cholla's strokes resemble Asian one-stroke calligraphy art. He has had art shown in galleries in Reno, Las Vegas, and Virginia City, Nevada. In June 2006 he had a showing at the New York City gallery Art at Large. The show was titled "Going Underground." Cholla even has his own website where people can enjoy viewing his art and watching him paint.

Renée's Cholla

The October 2005 issue of London's *Art Newspaper* acknowledged Cholla in its "Art Market" section by ranking him as the fourth animal artist in the world. The top three animal artists the article named were Congo the chimp, Tillamook Cheddar the dog, and the Thailand elephants.

Martha Stewart also recognized Cholla's talent by having my husband and me on her television show to exhibit Cholla's art, along with video footage of him creating one of his masterpieces at his easel.

Cholla is a horse who does not need to hide his emotions. I rarely say no to him, but when I do, he knows that I mean it. He respects me yet is pure and completely free to express himself. I guess that is part of the reason why he has become such an accomplished artist.

As a dancer I know that art manifests itself as we create. Art is an expression of intelligence, and Cholla's intelligence is remarkable. His soul is alive. But where do this ability and talent come from? Possibly he tunes in to cosmic frequencies as he paints. Perhaps it is the essence of other artists — maybe psychic premonition, reincarnation, or ancestral memory — that filters through his consciousness. I can only speculate. Wherever it comes from, Cholla's artistry is pure and magnificent.

Meditation

Have you ever met a horse with artistic or creative tendencies? What did this horse teach you about your own potential?

Pajaro, the Horse Who Runs with the Wind

Caroline Kane Aguiar
Ensenada, Baja California, Mexico

*H*orses have been an important part of my life since I was about eight years old. My teenage years were chaotic, but no matter what was going on at the time, I always found a sense of peace, a calm within myself, when I was around horses. Their strong presence and gentle souls had an incredible healing effect on me. At almost every major turning point in my life, whether it involved an event or a decision I had to make, the right horse would appear to help me when I needed him most.

I met my husband, Raul, through horses. At the time, I was managing a boarding stable in the San Fernando Valley, a suburb of Los Angeles. He had come from a horse background, having spent many summers on his Uncle Kiki's cattle ranch in their home of Baja California, Mexico. Raul and I were married, and five years later we moved to Baja with our two children, Ricky and Christine.

Our family began visiting Uncle Kiki's ranch again and riding horses. Although horses were low on our priority list after the birth of our two children, by the time Ricky was eight and Christine seven, both could handle a horse pretty well. We took rides together on the weekends while exploring the mountains that surrounded the ranch. It was a wonderful chance for the four of us to spend time together and relax from our hectic lives in the city. We spent hours exploring the land. Our horses' hooves were sometimes the only sounds we heard as their sure-footed steps echoed along the manzanita-scented trails. Nature seems to give a person a healthy sense of well-being. It opens up your senses to a whole other world. Raul and I wanted Ricky and Christine to experience that while they were growing up — to learn that there is more to life than computers and video games.

I started hearing Raul talk of a new business venture — a guest ranch. Before long he and Uncle Kiki had become business partners. We built cabins and started promoting the ranch. It was to be a guest ranch where people could ride horses, enjoy cattle drives and camp-outs, or just relax around the fire pit and shed their layers of stress from city life. Two years later we officially opened the guest ranch. Soon people were making reservations one year in advance to vacation there. Horses were definitely back in our lives.

This was nine years ago, and I am still amazed at how fortunate my husband and I are to have made such a wonderful life for our family. We spend every weekend on a beautiful ranch. We ride all the time. And we meet the most fascinating people along the way. Ricky and Christine have benefited tremendously, Ricky more so because he was older and more able to help than his younger sister. Early on he learned what it meant to work. At the age of sixteen he could handle more responsibility than any other teenager his age. Today, if for any reason Raul would be unable to do so, eighteen-year-old Ricky could take care of all the preparations for a group and lead the trail rides. He is an excellent rider.

After opening the guest ranch, I kept wondering what else was in store for us. And then I met Pajaro.

Pajaro means "bird" in Spanish. I remember spending hours, even days, trying to think of a new name for him. As I grew to know him better, I realized Pajaro was a perfect name for him. It was four years ago that I first laid eyes on this six-year-old bay gelding. He was a former racehorse and looked it too. At 15.5 hands, Pajaro had a nice conformation, a sleek body, and toned muscles, with long, powerful hind legs that meant he could *really* move.

In Mexico among the cowboy community, the cowboys hold periodic races along the beach. They take these races quite seriously by wagering high stakes. The loser has to hand over not only the purse money but his horse as well. A cowboy told us that Pajaro had been doing well until he placed second in his last race. The winner didn't want another horse and sold him to a cowboy who later came into financial troubles. That was when the cowboy heard that Raul was looking for a horse.

Raul looked at Pajaro and rode him but wasn't very impressed. I told Raul I wanted to ride Pajaro. He was hesitant about my riding a strange horse and tried to talk me out of it. The cowboy told us that the horse was quite a handful because he hadn't had proper training. When these racehorses are broke, they are taught to run like the devil in a straight line. Getting them to stop is difficult. The cowboy agreed with Raul that I should be very careful.

When I swung my leg over Pajaro's back for the first time, I felt confident and in control. We went for a relaxed ride around the hills. Until we got to the barley fields, I was amazed by the horse's calm manner and his willingness to go wherever I guided him. Suddenly he began to prance and toss his head. It was obvious that he wanted to run.

Anyone who knows horses also knows that it is not safe to be too confident on a strange horse, no matter how gentle he seems. I knew that, but something inside told me that I had nothing to worry about. Being a speed demon myself, I gave Pajaro more rein, and we broke into a nice lope. This quickly turned into a fast gallop, which escalated into a dead run as he strained on the bit, asking for more freedom. I felt an unbelievable power under me as, little by little, I let the reins out. I bent down close to Pajaro's neck and gave him his head. A bolt of energy rippled through his body and mine as he gathered himself and shot ahead. We ran with the wind, and both of us loved it. If for an instant I had looked down at his side, I would not have been a bit surprised to see he had sprouted wings. It felt like we were flying.

When it came time to stop, because we were running out of barley field, I pulled back on the reins as hard as I could. Pajaro fought me until I finally managed to slow him down. I knew that if we bought this horse, he would definitely need a lot of work. Much to the cowboy's delight, though, we bought Pajaro that same day. Raul was not entirely convinced about Pajaro, and he warned me that I might be taking on too much. But my gut instinct told me this would not be the case.

I started riding Pajaro on the trail rides with our groups. We worked on being calm and quiet while walking at a slow, easy pace. Sometimes we rode at the front of the group and sometimes in the back. It took a while before Pajaro began to understand that being in the back of the pack didn't mean he was going to lose the race.

The more I rode him, the more we grew to know each other. I began noticing certain qualities about him that really sparked my interest. He was agile and sure-footed. He could turn on a dime and was extremely quick. These were exactly the qualities needed for a barrel-racing horse. In barrel racing, the horse and rider race against the clock as they run the barrel pattern, which is a large triangle with three barrels set up within ninety feet of each other. It requires speed, agility, and intricate rider-horse communication at all times.

My dream was to compete in barrel races. Many of us have desires we keep tucked away in the backs of our minds. As a kid, sometimes I would watch barrel racers on television. My adrenaline would begin to flow as those girls shot around the barrels and raced for the finish line. As soon as I found out there were barrel races at the rodeos in Baja, my interest sparked once again. I knew Pajaro had the ability. The only problem was, neither he nor I knew how to go about training for this type of race.

I bought a book on training barrel horses, set up three barrels in our familiar barley field, and went to work. Poor Pajaro was in shock the first few months of practice, and so was I. He had been trained to run in a straight line. Now I was asking for lead changes and fig-ure eights. At first Pajaro resisted, and I became frustrated and unsure of myself. But we kept at it. We patiently worked together — he on figure eights and I on correct leg cues and reining maneuvers. After three months we were ready for our first race. Or so I thought.

We finished our first barrel race in a whopping thirty-six sec-onds flat. Nobody runs the course in thirty-six seconds. Anything over twenty-five seconds is a disaster, with nineteen seconds consid-ered average. All that hard work had gone down the drain. I felt very discouraged.

The evening of our first barrel race, after I finished tending to

Pajaro, I sat down in the corner of his stall and moped. He eyed me while munching alfalfa leaves. Then he walked over to where I sat. He lowered his head, sniffed my hair, and stood quietly. I could feel his warm breath on my head. This strong yet gentle soul towered above me, his presence reassuring and calming. It was as if he wanted me to relax for a while and enjoy the moment.

Caroline and Pajaro

I closed my eyes. I don't remember how long I sat there, but when I opened my eyes again a wave of inspiration washed over me. We had come this far and were going to go further, together. After my moment of realization, Pajaro remembered the alfalfa and slowly moved back to his hay flake. I jumped up, already planning another strategy for our next barrel race.

One year later Pajaro and I were doing times between eighteen and seventeen seconds. We were clocking times along with the other women, who had been barrel racing for years. We never placed first, but we competed with the best of them. Thanks to his natural athletic ability, Pajaro didn't once knock down a barrel.

Since our barrel-racing days, Pajaro taught me much about my capabilities and myself. He taught me to follow my dreams, to work hard, and to achieve my goals. Training Pajaro, taking care of him, driving out to the stables twice a day to feed and clean his stall while working and taking care of two kids and a husband were the hardest things I ever had to do. A tough dose of reality combined with commitment and responsibility taught me well, thanks to Pajaro.

I believe riding and training with Pajaro helped me with my human relationships as well. He taught me to have patience and understanding with the ones I love. Now these two qualities seep into my life on a daily basis, when I find that extra ounce of patience and understanding after I think I have none left. I was teaching something totally foreign to him, but his willingness to please always shone through, even on days when his patience was thin and I was ready to give up. I would remember the great effort he was making for me and understand his frustration. Those were the days we both needed to take a break. We would ride for an extra long time in the hills for a much-needed change of scenery.

Pajaro and I don't race anymore. Now we ride with groups on the trails, chase cattle, and have fun together with an occasional run through the barley fields. Pajaro never enjoyed running barrels, but all that time he did it for me, and I am very grateful.

Sometimes our guests comment about how well Pajaro and I work together on the trail. They ask me what it is I'm doing with the horse. My husband has asked me this also, and I honestly don't know.

I think Pajaro and I have established a unique relationship. We understand each other, and nowhere do I feel more safe, more in my place, than astride his back. We have ridden long hours at a time through areas most people would hesitate to enter. I would confidently ride him to the ends of the earth if I had to, and I know he would get me there. I trust him completely, and I believe he trusts me. We work as a team. I think that is what people are seeing.

I have no doubt that when I am fifty we will still be riding over the mountains. We'll be a bit older, a bit stiffer in the joints, but we will still be together. I hope Pajaro knows how grateful I am to him for the great joy he has brought into my life.

Sometimes trainers and clinicians tell me that Pajaro isn't trained properly. He's a hothead. He can't side-pass or stop once he gets going. I just laugh and wave them away. I know how to keep Pajaro calm under pressure. I know what makes him tick. I'm the one who rides and loves him, not the clinicians and the trainers. I believe Pajaro, too, knows what is important about him.

One of the things I give Pajaro in return for his devotion to me is a chance to indulge in his love of running. When we are out riding and come to a wide-open space, Pajaro prances and tosses his head. It is his way of telling me that this is a good spot for a run.

How can I deny him? It is part of his spirit, the spirit of a horse, to run wild and free, to run with the wind. I am so glad I am allowed to share that with him, to let him fly like the bird he was meant to be.

Meditation

Has a horse given up something important to be with you? What has this shown you about selfless service?

The New Animal Alchemy

Amelia Kinkade
North Hollywood, California

The big iron gates slammed ominously behind me as the high-ranking official, the assistant adjutant, ushered me through the guarded private entrance, closed off to the public. It was my second visit to Buckingham Palace. During my first trip the autumn before, I had stood outside the front gates with the rest of the tourists, popping off snapshots, gaping at the spectacle from a distance, separated from the Queen's abode by imposing guards and big, black wrought-iron fences.

Now, barely five months later, I was inside those gates. My floral scarf whipped in the wind, so I nervously tucked it into my beige cashmere jacket to sop up the trickle of perspiration dripping down my chest. I hurried to keep up with the quick stride of the captain of these barracks, the assistant adjutant. It was a cool, crisp May day in London, a far cry from the 100-degree-plus temperatures I weathered in my native Los Angeles, but the last time I'd sweated like this, I'd been in a Beverly Hills spa, inhaling eucalyptus. I tried to remember to breathe. As I strode across the palace yards, flanked on both sides by British military officials, the cheerful sun beamed down on my flushed cheeks and lit the castle walls in pink pastel hues, like a watercolor painting. Every ounce of my courage and talent was about to be tested.

As a "corporate enabler" and international translator with a growing reputation for solving problems in management and creating cooperative teamwork, I'd been brought in as a troubleshooter on "official royal business." The military was having problems with a few of its personnel. Some of their older employees were growing discontented, and a few of the new foreign recruits were having difficulties adjusting to their environment and workload. None of these employees spoke English.

I was met by many more men in brass-buttoned uniforms who saluted me and clicked the heels of their shiny black boots as I passed. The assistant adjutant ushered me inside the building and down a long corridor, lined with cubicles where employees worked.

Amelia communicating with a horse

The adjutant said, "I'm not sure we picked the best time for you to talk to them. We just served them lunch."

"It's okay," I said nervously. "Maybe they'll speak to me while they're eating."

"This is Captain Harris," the adjutant said. "His performance has been excellent for years, but lately he's been quite argumentative. He seems to have lost his spirit. He's not nearly old enough to consider retirement, but he seems a bit discontented with this job. Ask him what the trouble is."

As I walked into Captain Harris's cubicle, he was facing the other way, eating a bowl of oatmeal. When he saw me, he did a double take, and then went back to his lunch.

"Oh, I thought you were a carrot," he said.

I was utterly bewildered. I'd worked with a number of mentally challenged employees in the past but no one had ever mistaken me for a carrot before.

"What?" I asked.

"Your sweater," he said. "It's my favorite color." I looked down to find I was wearing a bright orange sweater under my jacket and the hot coral color did actually form the elongated triangle-shape of a carrot.

"Well, his peripheral vision is not very good," I said, jotting notes in my notebook, "especially not on his right side."

"Did you bring me any carrots?" he asked.

"No. I'm sorry, I didn't. I understand you haven't been feeling yourself lately. Are you having problems with your diet?"

"It's very boring," he said, moving over to a plate of dry-looking salad.

"And your digestion?" I asked.

"Not very good since my co-worker left. Have you seen the cat?"

"No, not yet. What color is it?"

"She's gray and white striped. She visits my cubicle at night. She's been cheering me since my friend got transferred."

"Do you know there's a gray and white cat in this building?" I asked the assistant adjutant.

"Oh, yes. That's Emma. I didn't know he liked her."

"Tell him everyone likes Emma. She does wonders for morale," Captain Harris told me.

"Ask him if he wants to retire," the assistant adjutant urged me.

"Of course not!" Captain Harris answered indignantly. "I'm one of the Queen's favorites! I've won many awards! I could never retire. It would disappoint her. We have to practice marching in the parade this Saturday and the entire team is counting on me to be in charge."

When I relayed the message, the assistant adjutant's eyes bulged.

"Yes!" he confirmed. "They have a practice on Saturday. Well, if he enjoys his work, and he's looking forward to the big event, ask him why he hasn't been able to concentrate lately."

"Your boss has been concerned about your performance," I prodded. "Are you not happy working here anymore?"

"I miss my friend. Bernard. They moved him into the cubicle on my left. We enjoyed working side by side and talking after work. The little cocky whippersnapper was so full of himself. He made me laugh and feel young again. I was just beginning to show him the ropes when they shipped him out. He got transferred up north to work in the beautiful countryside while I got stuck down here. I want to go up there too. Or I want him to come back. I miss him terribly. We need to be together."

When I relayed this message, the assistant adjutant was visibly shaken.

"Please tell him to bring Bernard back," Captain Harris said.

"He's lonely," I said to the adjutant. "He missed the boy who used to stand on his left. He gives me the name Bernard. He says Bernard has been shipped up north to the beautiful countryside to work, while the Captain has to stay down here all alone." The adjutant was speechless. When he found his voice, he said excitedly:

"Yes, it's true! There was a boy standing on his left named Bernard! I never knew he meant that much to the Captain. Bernard got transferred up to Prince Charles's hunting facility in the Midlands a couple of weeks ago. It's true! The countryside is green and beautiful, and all these boys have more fun up there hunting in the woods. We ship them back and forth so they get a change of scenery.

We thought the Captain was too old to want to do that anymore. Bernard! That's astonishing! How could he possibly tell you his name! Whoever would dream he could call his friend by name!?"

What's wrong with Captain Harris? Why wouldn't he know his best friend's name? Is he senile? Is he deaf?

No. He's a horse. Captain Harris is one of the royal procession horses of Queen Elizabeth II. I was invited to Buckingham Palace in May of 2002 to work with the Queen's household cavalry just as the horses were training for Her Majesty's Royal Jubilee. A few days later, I was further honored by an invitation to Prince Charles's hunting facility where I got to meet Bernard in person and give him a kiss on the nose. Animal lovers, have no fear. Both boys were joyfully reunited shortly after my visit. Welcome to the new animal alchemy where all animals — two- and four-legged alike — can "talk" to each other, quietly, peacefully, and without misunderstandings.

Meditation

What does the friendship of horses show about the value of loyalty?

Ladigan's Tears

Carman Colwell-Baxter
Otis Orchards, Washington

When Ladigan came to live in the pasture next to my land, he was ten years old and his mother was seventeen. He was a chestnut brown mustang–quarter horse, his face distinguished by a blazing star on his nose. I boarded horses at my place, and Ladigan always stood at the fence, watching them. I would talk to him as I walked around my field in the mornings. I always asked if he was having a good day. He would nod yes.

In summer of 1990 someone gave me an eighteen-month-old Alaskan malamute named Nina. A vision in black and white, she had a smiling white face and white legs, with black on her head, back, and the top of her wagging tail. She loved horses, so I would put her collar and leash on, and we would walk in the field with the horses.

One day Nina went to the fence and barked at Ladigan. He came over and put his head down to her nose. It looked like they were mentally talking to each other. First one then the other would shake their heads. Then they stopped abruptly, and Nina wanted to go back into the house.

After that day Nina and I went out every evening to see Ladigan. The dog and the horse always performed the same ritual. These conversations went on until Nina died in April 2004.

For two weeks I grieved privately for Nina before I went to visit Ladigan again. First he looked at me, then he searched with his eyes into the distance, toward my house. I told him that Nina had died. He seemed to understand as he shook his head up and down, then put his mouth on my arm and nuzzled it. I continued to visit with him every day. His compassion helped to lift my spirits over losing Nina.

In October of that same year I had surgery and was very ill. It was ten days before I could venture outside. When I did, Ladigan was there to greet me at the fence. He whinnied. I waved to him, but he kept on whinnying. I walked to him, and he put his head over the wire fence for me to scratch, as I always did. This time I sensed something different about him. To my surprise, I noticed large tears trickling down his sad face. For some reason I said, "Ladigan, don't cry for you will be seeing Nina and your mom soon." I was referring to Nina's recent death and the fact that his mother had died in 1993 at the age of thirty.

It was five days before I went outside again. Each day, though, I looked out my windows and saw Ladigan in his field. On the sixth day after my last walk, I didn't see Ladigan and assumed he was in the barn.

The next week, when Ladigan still wasn't in the field, I asked his owner about the horse. He told me that Ladigan had died. In fact, the tearful horse had died the same day that I had assured him he would soon be with Nina and his mother again.

His owner said that he still could see Ladigan in the field. I confided that I had also seen Ladigan. I was shocked to learn that my horse friend had died weeks ago, because I had continued to see him in the field all those days.

I know that when we care the most about our horses, they also care about us. Ladigan wanted to make sure his owner and I saw him. This way we would know that although he was gone physically, he was with us in spirit.

Meditation

Has a horse or other animal ever visited you in a spiritual way?

Wee Lass and Promise

Sharon Kay Roberts
Huntsville, Arkansas

*M*y lifelong love of horses and ponies turned from personal to altruistic in 1998 when I transformed my five rural acres into a breeding and training facility for Personal Ponies, Ltd. This nonprofit organization, active in forty-nine states, exists solely to enrich the lives of special children. Its founder, Marianne Alexander, had long observed a special bond that could exist between a pony and a child with special needs or a terminal illness. Her enthusiasm quickly infected me, and I soon found myself accepting the additional work of being Arkansas director for the charity.

As a breeder and trainer for this all-volunteer organization, I know that each pony I accept means an additional strain on my working-woman's budget. Ponies must be fed, cared for, and trained a year or longer. Even so, I often receive offers to add to my collection.

One day a friend, Barbara, called. She breeds and raises miniature horses to sell as show animals and offered me what she described as "a little mare with a lovely disposition who looks too much like a pony to do well in the miniature horse show ring." I agreed to come to her farm and see the pony.

While United Kingdom Shetland ponies have the personality traits and conformation that make them ideal as companion animals, they are rare in the United States. Importing purebreds is very expensive. So I am always willing to take a look at American Shetlands and miniature horses, both of whom share ancestors of UK Shetlands for their disposition and conformation.

As I drove to Barbara's miniature horse farm, I found myself wondering if the mare she offered would have the necessary temperament to be placed with a child. To make a good companion pony, the horse should be gentle and sweet and love attention. For generations the UK Shetlands have lived on an island without large predators, so they have very low flight instinct and do not frighten easily. This makes them safe for small children to handle. Too, I wondered about her warning that the mare came with her own companion, another pony. She had been reluctant to give any more details, saying only, "You will see for yourself."

My heart skipped a beat, or maybe several, when I met Promise, the pony she offered to me on the phone, and the pony's companion, Sahara (soon to be renamed Wee Lass). Sahara was badly misshapen with dwarfism. Her head was too large for her small body, and her legs were too short and malformed. She was an ugly duckling with no chance of ever becoming a swan, or so I thought at the time.

My folks used to comment on the personality quirk in me that led to my always choosing the runt of the litter whenever we picked out a puppy for a pet. Now my heart went out to this supremely ugly little pony, Sahara.

My friend didn't have to point out to me that the two mares shared a special love. The lovely mare Promise treated the dwarf mare Sahara as her special friend, always hovering protectively near her. Sahara never left Promise's side, reveling in the comfort and protection of a true friend.

The love the mares shared overwhelmed me. I could only say thanks and load the two pals into my small pony trailer. Instinctively I knew that I would never be able to separate Promise and the dwarf pony I now was calling Wee Lass, who would have too many health problems due to her dwarfism. Placing her with a deserving child along with Promise would create an additional burden for a family coping with special medical needs.

What had I gotten myself into now? Somehow, my worries didn't seem to matter as I basked in the warm glow of the two horses' love.

My friend Brea Poyner, who eventually succeeded me as PPL Arkansas director, helped me to find a purpose for the inseparable pair. Together we developed the Ambassador Program. Promise and Wee Lass went through the Delta Society's rigorous testing and became Delta Pet Partners with Brea and me. Delta Pet Partners allow people the chance to help their communities while enjoying the companionship of their animals. Pet Partners are welcomed in hospitals, nursing homes, schools, and similar situations. The focus of our Ambassador Program was to reach grade school children with the message of tolerance and acceptance.

Using the book *It's Okay to Be Different* by Todd Parr (Megan Tingley Books, 2001), we read to the children when we visited schools with the two horses. The book combined fun and instruction. Each page had a simple illustration and text, such as a child in a wheelchair with the words, "It's okay to have wheels."

The children loved to interact with us and tell how they and their best friends differed — hair or skin color, wearing designer jeans or not, or having a physical limitation. When so young, children have not yet learned prejudice. That is a lesson that takes years of careful nurturing by intolerant elders.

While the book and discussions were going on, Promise and Wee Lass would stand quietly tied to the trailer. After the book was finished, Brea or I would tell the children that sometimes when we see someone who is different from us, we might feel "funny in the tummy" and not want to go play with them. If anyone felt that way, we said that we might need to put one of the ponies back into the trailer. Wee Lass was a dwarf and therefore was different, and someone might feel "funny in the tummy" around her. The children would then protest at the idea of putting Wee Lass away.

Soon all the kids and ponies would be interacting. The ponies loved the attention and had an instinctive ability to relate to each child on the level he or she needed. To some children they gave slobbery pony kisses. With fearful children they would stand ever so still, allowing the child to take the amount of time needed for stroking velvety hair or touching a soft muzzle. With these visits, my special ponies taught the children that indeed it is okay to be different.

As our Ambassador Program developed, I was pleased to find that the ponies first taught me about accepting differences. Then they inspired me to find a way for them to teach their valuable lesson of love and tolerance to many children of varying abilities.

Wee Lass all too soon succumbed to the many health complications of dwarfism, and her loving friend, Promise, apparently died of a broken heart. Other teaching teams — Missy and Dandy, Grey Mist and Wee Princess — followed Wee Lass and Promise, but none of them seemed to share that very special love that was the genesis of the program to teach children.

My little ugly duckling had proved to be a beautiful swan all along. I just needed to learn to see with my heart. She was my teaching pony, and she taught me skillfully.

Meditation

What have horses taught you about honoring an individual's uniqueness and your own?

To Love Full Circle

Jo Ann Holbrook
Mount Vernon, Indiana

A proverbial city girl, I longed for a horse and rode broomsticks up and down the sidewalk, dreaming. I wished on every birthday cake and even coerced my husband, Gil, to promise *before* we were married that when the time and finances allowed, I would have a horse.

We had to sell our first horses when Gil lost his job. An animal's health and welfare is far more important than possession. Once we reestablished ourselves, we purchased a half-Morgan, half–quarter mare. She died within six weeks, after suffering from bloodworms, which wreaked havoc on her intestinal tract.

I was emotionally drained from loving horses and losing them. Could I start it all over again?

About that time a local horse trader called and urged me to meet Dan, a four-year-old grade horse. The trader said that Dan needed a good home and a gentle person. Being aware that I had sold my horses in the past, he also knew I needed to have a horse again, and Dan and I would be good for each other.

As the weeks passed, I went out to watch Dan run the pasture like a mustang. He had an intimidating wildness about him, yet he began to grow on me. At our first meeting Dan galloped past repeatedly while I watched him at the fence. With each pass, he inched closer to me. I could tell that he was as curious about me as I was about him.

Eventually I asked the trader if Dan could accompany us to Alabama where my husband had planned a vacation. I would ride for nine days. If I liked Dan, I would buy him. If not, I'd return him. So began my biggest learning experience from an animal.

Dan was no usual horse — not perfect or beautiful to those who didn't know him. Other people failed to notice Dan, especially when he accompanied purebred quarter horses with better conformation. A simple Heinz 57 variety of backgrounds, he was, to me, more than perfect and beautiful. He was a friend and companion. All of my childhood dreams reached fulfillment, wrapped up in his soft muzzle and gentle heart.

If I was giddy, Dan would be too. When I was sad, his bottom lip quivered and trembled as if he felt the need to cry because I did.

At 14.5 hands, Dan was the right size for a trail horse. A blond sorrel with flaxen mane and tail, he shone in sunlight with flamelike golden hairs appearing on his sleek coat and mane. He bore a small white diamond in the center of his forehead. His only white mark, it glowed in the dark, always revealing his approach to the barn at breakneck speed. A simple whistle brought the dancing diamond right to me, where he would halt and place his head directly upon my chest, listening to the beat of my heart.

Dan had been gelded right before I bought him. Only one person had owned him until a neighborhood man bought him because he thought the horse looked flashy. He rode Dan with his abusive hands for six weeks, using a crop to smack the horse's neck and head and spurs to gouge him onward. By the time Dan came to me he was a nervous wreck. According to his previous owner, Dan had only been green-broke, which meant that he had learned to accept someone on his back without understanding what it meant to be ridden.

Dan was indeed green, and scared of everything. Just like me. I had never trained or ridden a horse this young. I only knew what was in my heart, and my heart told me that Dan needed kindness and patience.

Whenever I approached him, Dan would tremble, his eyes turning wild. To gain his trust, I spent almost a year walking toward him in the pasture and offering treats. If I rode with anyone who yelled at a horse or popped the reins, Dan would go to pieces as if he were the one in trouble. More than once I left riding groups where someone was fussing at a horse just to keep Dan calm, to assure him all was well in our world. Each time he was frightened, it taught me to have patience.

While Dan tolerated traffic, bulldozers, and tractors, he panicked if a person walked out of a garage or opened a door. If he saw someone doing one of these things, he took off at breakneck speed, fleeing, as all horses do, from what he feared. By the time I managed to stop him, we might be in the middle of a farmer's three-hundred-acre field, with me calling, "Whoa, Dan Boy, whoa. It's okay. It's okay."

Eventually Dan grew so trusting that I was able to take him to visit Boy Scout and Girl Scout troops and do demonstrations. I watched as children fed him minute amounts of grain from small hands. They could pick up his feet and touch him anywhere. He always loved their attention. He had learned to trust me. But he also now, after our years together of meeting other horses and people, had learned to trust them too.

Through the years Dan toted many who confessed they were afraid of horses. He was always careful not to frighten them. He became a symbol of trust for children and elderly alike, carrying those from six months of age to eighty years with purpose and dignity in his walk. Years after I bought Dan, our veterinarian said, "I don't know what you've done with this horse, but I believe I could do open heart surgery on him without the anesthesia." Dan was one of the most trusting horses he had ever seen. Yet it had taken years to undo the cruel damage another human had inflicted on him in only six weeks.

Because of Dan's past, filled with impatience and abuse by his previous owner, I wanted to raise one horse in my lifetime from birth. This is why we had Dantu (pronounced *dan-too*), who was born on our minifarm when Dan was twenty-five. Since Dantu was born of a stallion from another farm, I joked that Dan was Dantu's godfather — there to oversee his future.

Dan and I would pony Dantu around the neighborhood, asking children to come and pet him and adults to give him treats. Neither Dan nor I wanted this young horse to ever be afraid of humans.

A regular Houdini, Dan taught Dantu his mischievous pranks, like how to take off Dantu's halter and bridle, how to untie ropes to let other horses loose, and how to open gates. And yet Dan also taught Dantu the things he needs to know to carry me into old age: how to safely climb a hill or slowly and cautiously descend it, how to step across a log, and how to linger in a cool creek.

Dan watched at the fence while I trained Dantu to be ridden, as if he had to make sure I was doing it right. It sometimes tugged at my heart when I'd catch him peering over the fence. He knew, and I knew that he knew: Another horse would fill my days but never take his place.

By the time Dan was twenty-eight years old, I had had him for over half my life. Early on I had told Dan that I would never, ever let him hurt. My husband, Gil, had also promised this horse that he would never have to leave us. Selling our horses had brought pain we could not repeat. No matter what the future held, Dan would be with us until he died.

We kept both of these promises. No matter how hard the times while raising our sons, we never gave Dan less care.

Until he turned twenty-five, Dan was never sick. One day he ate too many weeds during a drought. His old liver was taxed and could not tolerate the weeds, so he got hepatitis. Also, by then Dan's internal body thermostat had quit working. In hot weather, when he could not sweat to cool, I would unsaddle him in caves or in creeks in Shawnee National Forest, and he would lie on the cool earth until the sparkle returned to his eyes. I always carried frozen packs and electrolytes to bring his body temperature down and to replace liquids he had lost. The vet had said Dan's inability to sweat was just a minor inconvenience that we could monitor.

Many a wonder was Dan, but never an inconvenience. We rode and enjoyed being together as long as possible. Our years together flew so quickly, a blink in life's journey.

Gil's love for Dan was as genuine as mine. Even though he was not a rider, he cared for Dan and could tell across our ten-acre pasture if anything was wrong. He was the one who noticed the lack of spark in Dan's eyes when the hepatitis hit. He was the one who awakened me one morning and said, "Honey, you'd better get up. Dan is lying in the mud. Something's wrong."

Dan would never lie in mud.

I don't know if it was colic, but he was in pain. I spent a couple of hours walking and assuring him while he did typical Dan things — nuzzling my face and hands. I could tell he was hurting. He would lie down and I would say, "No, Dan, don't roll." Rolling when a horse has colic or when stressed can twist an intestine, initiating extreme pain or even death. In response to my

Jo Ann's Dan

pleas, instead of rolling he lay flat with his eyes watching me. As his pain subsided, he got up, trotted to the end of the pasture, and whinnied loud and long while looking down the road. Returning to me, he stopped and put his head into my chest — the way he often said that he loved me. I saw the knowing look in his eyes. I felt Dan cry with me as vividly as if his tears were dripping onto my cheeks. Our time had come to an end, and each of us knew it.

Dan's closest horse friend, Handy, a wine-colored roan quarter mare, lived a half mile away. Always a talker, Dan would announce his coming so Handy would know we were near. That morning when Dan was so sick, every time he trotted to the pasture gate, I believed that he was telling Handy he was leaving. Dan had always said hello; this time it was good-bye. It was Dan's way.

I looked into Dan's eyes. They were always the key to knowing his health. They glowed when he ate a peach, when I yelled for him to come, when it was time to load up for a new adventure, and when I called him to supper. I had seen that light for all these years, while Dan fulfilled my dreams and made me complete. Now the light in Dan's eyes was dimming.

Gil and I decided it was time to keep our promises — that Dan would not have to hurt and that he would be with us until he died. We had to let him go.

Sometimes we must come full circle in life. It is painful and seems unfair that we must let go of what we love the most. Yet our promises must be kept, for they are a most important part of love.

I knelt down, cradling Dan's head in my hands while the vet helped us fulfill our promises. I said good-bye and thank-you to a horse who had become one of the most important loves of my life. I watched the light fade from his eyes. I felt his love and gratitude and knew that he felt mine.

For many weeks I physically ached for his smell, his touch, and the sight of him. Then on one coal-dark night, when the horses were called to the barn, an old familiar Dan-ache tugged at my heart. This is when I saw his small, white diamond moving randomly, as if in tease. I felt his presence as surely if he were standing beside me, putting his head to my chest. He continues every so often to tell me all is well in our world and that I will never hurt from the loss of him.

Dan lived with us until Dantu was four and well trained. I ride Dantu today in all the old familiar places where Dan and I spent time. Now and then, when Dantu playfully removes his halter or bridle, I feel contentment. Dreams do come true, and sometimes when I look in Dantu's eyes, I see a light. It comes from his heart. I often know that light in Dantu's eyes is Dan's way of saying all is well in our world.

Meditation

Who have been the full-circle loves in your life? What could you do today to remember them?

Thanks to a Special Horse, I'm a Real Investment

Janet L. Roper
Shorewood, Minnesota

*D*id you ever have a childhood dream that you carried into adulthood? I did. I desperately wanted a horse. Not just any horse, but the perfect horse. This horse would allow me to be a bareback rider at the local circus. This horse would be a palomino mare, more beautiful than Trigger, and would love me as much as I loved her.

As I grew into an adult, I kept adding to my vision. Not only would she be a pale gold color, she would be mellow, between the ages of twelve and fifteen years, and measure 14.3 hands (fifty-nine inches). Adulthood naturally brings with it the wisdom of experience, and when I grew up I realized that my love and respect for horses far exceeded my capabilities as a horsewoman. So I gave up my idea of riding bareback in a circus. By the time I was in my mid-forties, I accepted that what I needed was a babysitter — a horse who did not spook, would take care of me, anticipate my every need, and keep me safe.

After checking out twelve prospective horses, I became doubtful that my dream would ever come to pass. None of the horses I inspected even come close to what had been claimed about them in the advertisements. And none had passed the prepurchase veterinarian check. Finally, I was on my way to see the last horse on my list. Being an optimistic person, I had high hopes for this one, still believing that I would find exactly the right horse.

It was obvious to me that the horse trader, who led a beautiful palomino mare into the ring, was unhappy that my trainer had accompanied me. As the trader mounted her, the mare, who was twelve years old and 14.2 hands, began to fidget and balk. "I can't remember the last time she acted like this," he said, after riding the horse for a while.

At last the mare calmed down and finished her moves nicely. However, as soon as my trainer mounted her, I knew this was not the horse for me. She definitely had a mind of her own and needed a secure, strong, and experienced rider. My hopes were dashed once more.

"You know, you might be interested in seeing another horse I have," the horse trader said as we were leaving the barn. "Though this horse is a gelding and a western pleasure show horse, he has a wonderful personality and is very well trained. Why not look at him since you are already here?"

Janet and Shiloh

The moment the horse emerged with the trader, it was apparent that this would not be the horse of my childhood dreams. For starters, this was a male and I had always wanted a mare. There he stood in the ring, at 15.3 hands, looking worried and uncertain, a very unsure five-year-old red sorrel. He carried himself nervously, looking around and holding his breath.

The initial ride went smoothly, with the trader's wife putting the horse through his paces. It also went smoothly when my trainer, Karen, rode him. Dismounting, she said, "Why don't you give him a try, Janet? He seems like he would be a good horse for you." I rode the horse, and again everything went smoothly. That ride cinched it for me — that and the fact that this was the fourteenth horse I'd seen. I was definitely burned out from horse shopping.

"How is his health?" I asked the trader. "Does he have any bad habits, like bucking or rearing?"

"No," he replied. "This horse is in perfect health, and I've never seen him buck or rear."

That was it. I was sold. Two days later I returned to pick up the horse named Ima Real Investment.

As my new horse and I elegantly promenaded into the barn where he would be stabled, everyone gathered to welcome us. It was then that I overheard two women on the side speaking to each other:

"I sure hope she hasn't bought that horse," said the taller woman.

"I know," said the other. "I heard on the western pleasure circuit that he has a reputation for bucking and rearing."

Oh, no, I thought. *How can this be?* With my ears burning, I promptly rechristened Ima Real Investment with the barn name of Shiloh. The name just came to me. Later, after having animal communication done with him, I came to believe that he had been a horse at the Battle of Shiloh in the Civil War and had returned to this lifetime.

Shortly after our arrival, I asked the trainer to assess Shiloh's abilities. As soon as she started to longe (exercise) the horse, he began bucking furiously, obviously frightened. Quickly this fear lathered him with sweat. Once the bucking stopped, he began racing fanatically on the line. Finally he became so exhausted that he stopped racing. At last the trainer cooled Shiloh down enough so that I could return him to his new stall.

Strangely enough I could identify with the exhausted, panicked horse. This was a new situation for Shiloh. His actions and the tension in his body showed me that Shiloh did not know what to expect from a new owner or situation. Who could blame him? He had already been through three owners and at least one horse trader in his very short life. He had no idea what the future held for him.

I too did not know what the future held for either of us. I realized, though, that I was incapable of handling his fears or behaviors.

Without thinking, I automatically put my hands on Shiloh's neck and began gently stroking and petting him. I could feel the tension flow from his body. As I stroked him, I spoke nonsensical words to comfort both of us. My hands strayed to his muzzle, where I could feel huge degrees of anxiety leaving as he exhaled. Suddenly I was aware of my hand in his mouth, massaging his gums.

As I massaged his gums, I had a startling revelation: I knew that we would learn to trust each other on our journey. I also recognized that by trusting each other, Shiloh and I would grow confident together as we became more secure in our own beings. At that moment I made a lifetime commitment to Shiloh. We would be together until death parted us. Little did I know what that commitment would mean.

Eight glorious years passed with Shiloh. Looking back, I can see that he made a similar commitment to me: to be my teacher, mentor, and friend in all aspects of horse ownership.

From the beginning it was like Shiloh and I had made vows in a marriage — for better or for worse. In those eight years we have been through a lot together, perhaps more than the usual. For example, one day when I entered his stall, Shiloh was in pain with a mysterious muscle ailment. He couldn't be touched, much less ridden. Later he developed lameness and hoof problems. Next he suffered from a severely injured hind leg when he got tangled in pasture wire. Then he somehow acquired a puncture wound in his neck.

Shiloh's left eye would occasionally become red and inflamed, but it was not until his mishap with the wire fence that he was diagnosed with equine recurrent uveitis, or moon blindness. Shiloh and I and his vet fought valiantly to save both his sight and his eye. Each day he needed a dose of eye medication and aspirin. In one severe flare-up he was treated with eye medication three times a day.

Every trip I made to the stable to care for Shiloh's eye took a minimum of seventy-five minutes. Eventually his eye became so photosensitive that he wore a fly mask, sometimes as long as fourteen hours a day. In normal paddock horseplay, fly masks are destroyed. I finally decided to turn him out into a round pen where he could be by himself. He got very lonely out there.

In spite of all the tender loving care and aggressive treatment, Shiloh's pain became chronic and continuous. With the help of the vet, I made the decision to have the horse's eye removed. Shiloh adjusted quickly to having only one eye. Daily, he celebrates his medication-free life in the pasture, greeting his friends with arched neck and tail held high.

With all the vet bills, medicines, tack, and treats that Shiloh has needed during our partnership, he has ironically lived up to his registered name, Ima Real Investment. The return on investment has been the love that developed between Shiloh and me. With his friendship, Shiloh has turned *me* into a real investment. I am now more confident in myself and my decisions. Having this sorrel gelding in my life has made my childhood dreams come true and is responsible for my own growing success story.

Meditation

What people or horses have not met your expectations but then wound up exceeding them in their own ways?

Take a Bow, Sparky

Pamela Jenkins
Henryetta, Oklahoma

A cool, crisp early morning, it was just right for horseback riding. I would soon be enjoying my first ride on Sparky, our new horse. Although a bit too small, the paint was a beauty to look at. A twelve-year-old gelding, Sparky was brown, black, and white with a flowing white mane and tail. What he lacked in size, he made up for with his personality and willingness to please.

I gave Sparky a kick, and he started to gallop as fast as his little legs could carry us. We were racing along happily when Sparky did the unexpected and slammed on his brakes, coming to a sudden stop.

I was so surprised that I didn't even have time to shout, "Whoa!" I went flying through the air and landed in a dusty heap on the hard ground.

Oh, I'm going to feel this tomorrow, I thought. I opened one eye and looked back at Sparky. He stood at attention with his ears forward, waiting for me to pull myself together. I couldn't see a bit of remorse in those big chocolate eyes.

I managed to stand up and brush the dust off my pants and shirt. My hands were skinned and bruised. I ached all over. "You ornery old hay-burner," I began to say while walking back toward Sparky.

Then I heard my father's voice from the barn. "Now, don't hurt that horse!" he yelled.

I stopped in midstride. Don't hurt the horse? How in the world could my father imagine that I could hurt this huge beast who had just flung me through the air with the greatest of ease? Even more, if my father had been standing in the barn's doorway and witnessed the whole thing, why wasn't he worried about *me*?

"You must have done something to make him stop like that," my father said. He walked over and patted the horse on the neck. Then he reached down and gave Sparky an affectionate pat on the chest too. What happened next left both of us speechless.

Sparky dropped his head and bent his knees. He extended one front leg and, like a courtly gentleman, gave a bow. My father and I were so surprised that several seconds passed before we both burst out laughing.

Sparky's past was a mystery. We knew little about the old horse except a vague reference by his previous owner to his former days as a trick-performing pony. As he was passed

Pamela and Sparky

from one owner to the next, his commands and cues were forgotten by all but Sparky himself. We never knew what surprises he would show us next.

By spending time with Sparky, my brother and I found out that when we tapped his knee, he would count to four by pawing the ground. He could bow and pray if we patted his chest and would sit when we patted his rump. He would curl his lip and nod his head up and down if we touched his mane. By accident, we discovered that touching Sparky's flanks caused him to rear up on his hind legs, but we were strictly forbidden by our parents to make him perform that feat. Hooves dangling over our heads seemed too dangerous, even if Sparky was gentle as a lamb with children.

Sparky loved people and enjoyed being the center of attention. He would follow us like a puppy around the barns when we did our chores, sometimes getting in our way. He seemed happiest when we stopped and scratched his neck. He greeted visitors with a nicker and a nod of his head. No other horse could outshine him when it came to the yearly parade in our hometown. Sparky pranced with the best of them.

Sparky also had a weakness — his sweet tooth couldn't be satisfied. His favorite treat was a sugar cube. We made sure to never visit the barn without a few of them in our pockets. Sparky would nuzzle and smell until he found the hidden sugar. He could hardly wait to crunch into its sweetness.

One winter day we were cleaning around the barn, and Sparky was standing nearby, enjoying our company. My mother wore her new winter coat. It had huge white buttons down the front. Sparky's eyes lit up in wonder at what he must have thought were the biggest sugar cubes he'd ever seen. Unable to resist the temptation, he trotted over and snagged a button between his long front teeth.

"Oh!" my mother exclaimed as she tried to move away.

Sparky wasn't about to give up and held on with dogged determination. My mother waved her arms while Sparky batted his big brown eyes, but he wouldn't let go. Finally, with a pop, the button came off.

Sparky worked the button around in his mouth. We could hear it rattling against his teeth. But no matter how hard he tried, he couldn't make it taste sweet. In disgust, he spat it out on the ground and laid his ears back. The look he gave us clearly said, "Now, that was a dirty trick to play on me!"

To this day I never think of Sparky without a smile coming to my face. He gave us years of devotion and companionship. And even into his old age, he continued to pull surprises out of his hidden bag of tricks, like opening the pasture gate and bringing us the bucket at feeding time.

Take a bow, Sparky. You were one in a million.

Meditation

Does Sparky spark your own childhood memories of special horses who brought an extra dose of love and laughter into your life?

Zeke and I: The Perfect Marriage of Dreams and Destinies

Lois Stanfield
Minneapolis, Minnesota

*H*aving ridden for most of my younger years, I began a search for my "dream horse," a young horse whom I could raise and ride into the international levels of dressage. While living in California, each weekend I would look at young horses, searching for the perfect one. On a working girl's salary, it was a crazy thing to do, but I continued my search anyway.

I was about to give up when one night I had a dream in which my inner spiritual teacher, the Dream Master, showed me that horses would be my flute, meaning involvement with horses would be my way of expressing divine love and creativity. So although I had been unsuccessful so far, I decided to continue my search. The very next day after having the dream, I went to see a couple of yearling colts. I fell in love with one of them. I told the owner, "I don't know why I am here. I don't have any money, but this colt is exactly what I'm looking for!"

The owner suggested, "Come look at his mother. Maybe you can ride her through the winter. Then in the spring you might be able to buy the colt."

I looked at the mare, Gel's Hope, as the owner had suggested.

She was a lovely, mahogany bay, thoroughbred mare and had produced some very nice foals. But I learned she was a dangerous,
unpredictable creature. The first time I rode her, she bucked me off
three times and then, as I lay in the dirt, reared and tried to come
down on top of me. I thought she was going to kill me. I was very
afraid, but instead of running away from the situation, I decided this
mare would be a challenge that could help me to grow both spiritually and as a horsewoman. I did not know at the time, but this mare
would help me learn how to become a kind of "horse whisperer" as
I grew to understand her and why she acted as she did.

I worked with her throughout the winter months, gaining her
trust and respect, and she ended up being the sweetest, most loving
creature. I changed her name to Jellybean. Six months after we first
met, we even entered a horse show, and she won.

Then it was spring, and I had to make the decision about buying her colt. The evening before I was to decide, after I had fed her,
she left her feed and came up to the fence where I stood watching
her. This was remarkable because this mare lived to eat. She spoke to
me, looking into my eyes for the longest time, like she was saying,
"I'm your horse." That night I dreamed she had a brand on her hip
that said, "WahZ." This is the name of my spiritual teacher. So I
decided it was a sign that the mare was right about being mine. Her
owners were kind enough to make it possible for me to buy her by
working off much of her purchase price doing jobs at their ranch.

Jellybean's Colt

It soon became clear to me that breeding Jellybean would be the
next step in the search for my dream horse. With this realization, I

went on a quest to find the right stallion. I searched for about a year and finally had to surrender to Spirit my desires for her perfect match. Then I had a dream in which I was looking at many stallions. Before I awoke from the dream, my spiritual teacher said, "Zorn."

Zorn had been a Spanish painter, but it was also the name of a Swedish Warmblood stallion who had recently been imported from Sweden. Although Zorn was young and unproven, I went to look at him. My heart opened wide. I knew instantly that he was the right horse for my mare, so I bred her to Zorn. He went on to become a national and international champion dressage horse.

While my mare was in foal, I would often ride her bareback in the foothills of the Santa Cruz Mountains. Leaning over, close to her big belly, I would sing to the baby inside her.

When the foal was born, the white star on his forehead glowed large and bright like a headlight. It was as if he were saying, "Here I am. It's me." He was big, dark, bouncy, friendly, and absolutely beautiful. Lucky me!

Usually when a foal is born, first he eats. He struggles to his feet to find his mother's teats and drink the milk. But when this foal was born, he didn't care about food. He just lay on the straw and listened to the sound of my voice. He had become used to hearing it while in his mother's womb. Because of his fascination with the sound of my voice, I named him Zikar, which means the spiritual practice of listening to the Sound Current, or the Voice of the Holy Spirit. I called him Zeke for short.

Before Zeke was weaned, I had an animal communicator come out to talk to him and his mother. Regarding Zeke, the communicator said, "I've never seen one so young and so sure of himself and what he wants to do in life." She indicated something I already had sensed: Zeke is a master horse and he just wanted to get on with fulfilling his purpose. As if to verify the fact that Zeke wanted to mature as soon as possible, while he was still a baby he used to seek out a big log in his pasture. He would stand on top of it, like a goat, to make himself taller. He always wanted to be big.

For the first year of his life Zeke, his mother, and I lived on a horse farm in the foothills of the Santa Cruz Mountains where I was the caretaker. After he was weaned I would take him for walks like a dog. The farm's owner nicknamed Zeke "The Little Prince" because he had such a regal presence about him. I had a little cabin on the property. Zeke's paddock was next to it. He liked to come to the window and squeak his nose on it when he wanted me to come out and play. Sometimes I would crank open the window and reach out to scratch him. I worked at home, and one warm summer afternoon I left my living room door open to let in a cool breeze. While sitting at my desk, I heard the clatter of little hooves on my front porch. I walked out of my office to find Zeke standing in the living room, checking things out.

At only ten months old, he saved another horse's life. One night I heard him calling and calling to me until I awakened fully. I went outside to find that the owner's yearling Hanoverian filly had gotten loose and tangled in some equipment. Her leg was slashed, and she was bleeding like crazy. None of the eight other horses on the premises called for help, only Zeke, my little hero. We immediately called the owner and the vet. The horse needed stitches and would have bled to death if Zeke had not come to her rescue that night.

When Zeke was two years old I moved him and his mother from

California to my new home in Minnesota. By then I needed to present him for his breed to the Swedish Warmblood Society. An inspection team came out to test and approve the young horses for registration in the breed. Zeke scored quite high in his testing, enough to qualify for stallion testing as a four-year-old.

I began to notice that he was spending more time standing up on his hind legs in typical stallion posturing. I realized that if he remained a stallion, I would probably lose my friend because he would have other things on his mind. Zeke, the soul, came to me in a dream and told me that being my companion was what he wanted. I realized then that it was fine with him to be a gelded horse. He could keep his focus on his purpose and would be happy.

Lois and Zeke (© 2006 Lois Stanfield/LightSource Images)

When he was nearly three years old Zeke got a lesson in humility. He liked to rear up as high as he could go, as if he were reaching for the stars. One time, when I had turned him loose in our indoor arena, which had nice, soft footing, he reared up so high he fell over backward. He wasn't hurt but just lay there for a few minutes in the deep sawdust. Then he blinked his eyes and got up. After that spill he became a little humbler. He learned to reach for the stars but to keep all four feet on the ground.

Zeke likes having an audience and is quite a show-off. When he was about four or five years old, just starting out under saddle, we

were at a clinic riding with a trainer from out of town. An audience
of other riders had come to learn by watching this trainer teach. I
asked Zeke to canter. He gently bucked, out of sheer exuberance.
When the audience laughed, he did it again, and he proceeded to
buck like a porpoise, leaping in and out of the waves, all the way
around our twenty-meter circle. The more his audience laughed, the
more he bucked.

Zeke Trains for Dressage

When Zeke was seven, a wonderful trainer who came to our barn reg-
ularly for clinics took an interest in Zeke and asked if I would send him
to his barn in Chicago for training. He kindly offered a discounted
price to help me with the expense. So Zeke went off to Chicago.

He was doing very well. But after he was there for several
months, I had a dream in which Zeke told me that his feet hurt. I
watched as he dragged them like he could hardly move.

I called the trainer and said, "Zeke needs to come home. Something is not right."

The trainer did not believe me because Zeke looked fine to him,
but we set things in motion to bring my horse back. Not long after
my dream the trainer called and said, "Zeke is lame."

The trainer had a vet come out to see Zeke, and his diagnosis
was that Zeke had a problem in the stifle, the horse's knee. They
tried every way to treat the stifle but without success. The vet said,
"I am sorry, but he is permanently lame. There is nothing we can do
for him. If you are lucky, he might make a nice trail horse."

After bringing Zeke home from Chicago, I asked another vet to
look at him. Remembering the dream in which Zeke showed me his

feet dragging, I asked the vet to check out the horse's feet instead of the stifle. He X-rayed his lower legs and found a bone chip in Zeke's left fetlock joint, a condition called osteochondrosis dissecans (OCD). Sometimes when horses grow too fast they develop these bone chips. Zeke's was the size of a grape. The chip was in a place that made shifting his weight back onto his haunches, as he was learning to do in upper-level dressage, very painful. He couldn't sustain the weight with his legs. Based on the vet's recommendation, I had arthroscopic surgery done to remove the bone chip.

Zeke was better than ever. After he recovered he went back into dressage training with a wonderful world-class trainer from Sweden, Hokan Thorn. It was a great blessing for us that Hokan had moved to Minnesota, and we were able to work with him full-time for a couple of years. Within a year Zeke was schooling at the Federation Equestrienne Internationale (FEI) level. In dressage there are different levels — training, first through fourth levels, then the FEI levels of Prix St. Georges, Intermediare 1 and 2, and then Grand Prix.

I was fortunate and worked hard to make it to the FEI level with my horse, because you have to train extensively and it is very expensive. I worked sixty to eighty hours a week to pay for the training and horse shows. During this exciting time period, when Zeke was showing at fourth level and Prix St. Georges, he had a short write-up in a national horse magazine, *Chronicle of the Horse*. Zeke won our region's championship fourth level and came in third at Prix St. Georges that year, 1995.

The winter of 1995–96, Zeke and I went to Wellington, Florida, with my trainer, Hokan, where they held the Olympic selection trials. I used up all of my savings to spend the winter there in full training. It was such an amazing experience, riding and training with some of the greatest horses and riders in the United States. For two months we had a little piece of heaven. I was at the stable every morning with my horse. We trained every day and watched these magnificent horses and riders who were long-listed for the Olympic Dressage Team. I never competed down there. Somehow I didn't want to and couldn't afford it, anyway. Competing was never really my dream. Mine was to achieve, to learn, to strive. It was Zeke who enjoyed competing.

By the time we returned from Florida, Zeke had progressed so much that when my trainer was going to Dressage at Devon in Pennsylvania the following fall — a large, prestigious dressage show held every September — he asked if he could take Zeke with him and I agreed. I preferred having Hokan compete with Zeke while I groomed and watched. It's like seeing your kid in the school play. Zeke was not a world-class horse, but he has tremendous heart, ego, and determination and is all business in the show ring. Zeke competed at Devon with Hokan against some very fancy international horse-and-rider combinations, and he won the championship at fourth level.

My goal of becoming a true horsewoman blossomed over the course of my training with Zeke. I grew to know what Zeke feels and thinks. Dressage is like a dance. You shift your weight slightly or twitch a muscle, and a horse knows to do a certain movement. But even more, dressage involves inner communication. You just think it, and the horse does it.

Zeke and I at Our Crossroads

At one point, when Zeke was twelve years old, I was growing tired of the training and competing and was going through some very tough times financially. Yet I felt that Zeke had not fulfilled his destiny, so I decided it would be best if I sold him. Selling him was incredibly hard for me, but I believed it was best for both of us at the time.

I sold him with the agreement that he would come back to me if the new owners did not want to keep him for any reason. They had a teenage girl, and they bought Zeke for her. He bonded with the girl immediately and loved her. Now I was out of the picture, even though I would sneak out to visit him sometimes.

With the coaching and guidance of a wonderful and compassionate local trainer, Zeke taught the teenager everything he knew about dressage. After a year the teenager became so good that she won an alternate seat on the Young Riders Team, which is like an Olympics for young people. And Zeke just loved it.

Not long after, the girl went off to college. The owners were going to sell him, so they contacted me to see if I wanted to buy him. By then I had moved back to California and arranged for Zeke to come to me there.

We did more training in California, and at about sixteen years of age he started to get a little stiff. His love for me is so great that he would withstand any pain and try not to tell me about it. He has so much heart that he'll keep trying and trying even if it hurts. But I could tell something wasn't quite right. I had an ultrasound done on his legs to see what was going on. This revealed that he had torn ligaments in all four legs. I was floored. Any other horse would have been crippled and not even walked out of the stall. But not Zeke.

I immediately took Zeke out of training, hand-walked him each day, and did infrasound therapy on his legs daily for six months until they were completely healed without even any scar tissue. So his career was still not over.

After this time we returned to Minnesota, where we are now, still together. He is twenty-one years old, but he still wants to do something, so we will start a new career in trail riding this summer. He will be like a cowboy exploring the countryside, the trails, and the meadows. A friend suggested I show him movies of cowboys with their horses so he will know what trail riding is all about.

My Lifelong Love

Zeke has become my lifelong love. He won't take his eyes off me when I am at the barn. After I arrive at the barn each day, he neighs at the top of his lungs, greeting me. I can't sneak into the barn on a quick errand without him knowing it. Zeke gives hugs by holding me with his head, the way a person would hold an orange under his chin. He's very gentle with the hugging, especially if he knows I'm not feeling well.

Horses are very sensual creatures, and Zeke loves to be touched and groomed. A lot of times when I am at the barn, I cannot talk to someone unless I have my hands on him. He'll reach over and nip me if I don't keep touching him.

When people ride seriously in competition, they need to get along or jell with their horse temperamentally. Zeke and I are a perfect match in temperaments. He has a sense of humor. When I've gotten a little uptight, he always does something to loosen me up. I might be bending over, cleaning his feet, and he reaches back to give me a nip on my rear end. Sometimes when I'm walking him, he comes up from behind and lifts me up with his nose.

When I am not at my best, Zeke never reacts. Yet there have been times when he would reach over and nip me, as if to say, "No, you are really wrong." I have not been the perfect person, but I think he is the perfect horse, and he puts up with me.

It has been a lifetime partnership with our ups and downs. I guess we are in our twilight years now, and people ask me, "Don't you want to get another horse so you can continue to ride and train?" I say, "No, I have Zeke. We are in it till the end. Our love affair has lasted longer than many marriages."

If people think of animals as "just animals," they won't recognize them as souls. I allow Zeke to have the space to become a greater being. Zeke and I have been gifts to each other. He had a purpose and a destiny, and I had a dream.

Meditation

What could you do to help a horse fulfill his or her purpose in life while achieving your dreams as well?

Ask Zeke

Dear Zeke,

I think my horse loves me, but I don't know for sure. She whinnies when she hears my voice. But maybe it's just because she knows I carry sugar cubes in my pocket for her. Do horses love people?

Sincerely,
Clueless

Dear Clueless,

Yes, horses love sugar.

Oh, that's right, you wanted to know about people. We love people too. Especially the ones who are kind to us and make us feel special. Horses have hearts as big as the sky. A horse will be your friend forever and will love you even when you don't love yourself so much.

Did I mention we love sugar too?

Sweetly yours,
Zeke

CHAPTER TWO

Healing and Health

I pray that gentle hands may guide my feet;
I ask for kind commands from voices sweet;
At night a stable warm with scented hay,
Where, safe from every harm, I'll sleep till day.

— Author unknown

*I*n 1996 the Children's Miracle Network chose thirteen-year-old car-accident victim Nikki Anderson to be Minnesota's representative of disabled children for its fund-raising telethon. The gig called for Nikki to be an honorary bat girl for the Minnesota Twins. Turns out, Nikki owed her newfound fame and maybe even her life to a horse.

When Nikki was taken from the accident to Gillette Children's Hospital in St. Paul, medical teams rushed to save her life, but after the surgeries and procedures to restore brain and body, she remained unconscious. According to "Nikki's New Life," an article by Peg Meier in the *Minneapolis Star Tribune*, Callie, the horse whom

Nikki considered to be hers but belonged to her aunt, visited the girl at the hospital. Meier writes, "Nikki, unconscious, was taken outside on a stretcher to meet Callie, who sniffed and licked her. A week later, St. Paul mounted patrol officers brought two of their finest, Bob and Major, for more nuzzling. Horses made repeated visits."

Lisa Anderson, Nikki's mother, says that after each horse visit Nikki made significant progress. She gave her first laugh and said her first word, *Mama*, after a dose of what family and friends called "horse slobber." Later Nikki recovered enough to go home and back to school while continuing to receive extensive therapy at Gillette.[1]

Equine assisted therapy, also known as hippotherapy, has become much more evolved than horse kisses but with similar results to Nikki's success story. The North American Riding for the Handicapped Association (NARHA) accredits centers nationwide to use equine activities for helping children and adults with physical, emotional, and learning disabilities. Currently 650 NARHA program centers in the United States and Canada serve 30,000 disabled individuals annually. According to the organization's website, the American Occupational Therapy Association and the American Physical Therapy Association recognize equine-facilitated therapy to be a valuable adjunct to traditional forms of therapy. NARHA's website says, "Because horseback riding gently and rhythmically moves the rider's body in a manner similar to the human gait, riders with physical disabilities often show improvement in flexibility, balance, and muscle strength. For individuals with mental or emotional disabilities, the unique relationship formed with the horse can lead to increased confidence, patience, and self-esteem."[2]

It appears that the equine-assisted therapy benefits both people and horses. A report published online by the American Veterinary Medical Association (AVMA) showed that Dr. Marie Suthers-McCabe, an associate professor of human–companion animal interaction at the Virginia-Maryland Regional College of Veterinary Medicine, devised a study with Dr. Lynn Albana to find out what effect equine-assisted therapy has on horses. In a pilot study of twenty-eight horses of fifteen different breeds, the veterinarian researchers took blood samples before the horses assisted in therapy sessions. They wanted to assess whether levels of cortisol, the "stress hormone," increased or not. They also set up video cameras to tape the horses before, during, and after sessions. They were looking for raised cortisol and other indicators of increased stress, such as head weaving.

At a presentation to the AVMA Annual Convention in 2004, Dr. Suthers-McCabe reported that although therapy horses work hard, especially to help physically disabled riders stay on the saddle, the horses' cortisol concentrations actually decreased by 82 percent after a therapy session. Since six of the horses in the study did have higher stress levels, though, she is hoping that continuing the study will offer results that help therapy program coordinators assess which horses are experiencing stress and burnout or are not suited to this type of work.[3]

A twist on the theme of horses helping to improve people's health is the relatively new practice of equine-assisted personal coaching as a method for self-improvement. The Animal Sentience website article "Horses Can Teach Us a Thing or Two" states, "Equine therapy is being used in leadership trainings, psychotherapy, chemical-dependency treatment, and other settings. Some programs are even designed for children. Participants sign up in pairs — a mother and her adolescent son wanting to improve communication, for example. Others, such as workplace teams, take the courses."4

Horses heal people and people heal horses. In researching this chapter, we came across wonderful people and organizations that are devoted to rescuing and healing horses. The Thoroughbred Retirement Foundation, for example, gives sanctuary to horses who are headed for slaughterhouses. The Black Hills Wild Horse Sanctuary offers shelter and grazing for 400 horses on 11,000 acres through which the Cheyenne River flows.5 A fenced-in wild horse sanctuary on the Outer Banks of North Carolina is home to herds of wild horses who are descendants of those left by sixteenth-century Spanish colonists. Throughout the country volunteers work tirelessly to save the lives of wild and unwanted horses. Congressional legislators and animal organizations such as the Humane Society of the United States, American Society for the Prevention of Cruelty to Animals, and Animal Humane Association have banded together to end the practice of slaughtering horses. It seems the least this country can do for creatures without whom the civilization and lifestyles of today would not have become possible.

In addition to all these formal ways to bring horses and people together for healing and health improvement, there are the individual, the spontaneous, the miraculous healings represented by stories in this chapter.

Who are these miracle-working healers of body, mind, and soul? And what happens when people are blessed to have the heart of a great horse beating in harmony with their own?

The Heart of Whitehorse

Sherril L. Green, DVM, PhD
Menlo Park, California

*F*or the fifteenth time in less than an hour, my beeper inter-rupted, buzzing like an annoying horsefly. I took my stetho-scope from my ears and strode to the phone, irritated that I couldn't seem to get a moment's peace.

"Dr. Green, your next case is here." The clerk's voice was efficient and businesslike. It didn't matter that it was getting dark outside and I'd been up for thirty-six hours straight. That I wanted to go home, to get out of here before the cold Canadian winds kicked up and it started snowing. How this appointment got on my schedule, I didn't know. My resident, I guessed.

"Which case?" I asked, looking at my watch.

"The Indian chief's horse. The old stallion with chronic weight loss."

I liked it when the appointment clerk defined my cases by their medical problem. I could translate the description into the time it would take to make my diagnosis-prognosis and then get some blessed sleep. "Old" and "chronic weight loss" predicted a poor out-come. This one shouldn't take too long.

I stomped into the exam room to find a bony white horse stand-ing quietly in the stocks. He pricked his ears and lifted his head slightly, inspecting me with intelligent, soulful eyes. His ribs were showing, and his muzzle was speckled with small black growths that I recognized as melanomas. Cancer.

I spun around to find his owner, Chief Cloudman, according to the name stamped on the blue card the hospital used for billing.

Chief Cloudman was skinny too, dressed in faded jeans, a denim shirt, cowboy boots, and black cowboy hat. His skin was brown but especially smooth for a man whom I guessed to be in his sixties. A turquoise stone hung from the lariat on his neck, but with his white ponytail, handlebar mustache, and striking blue eyes, he didn't look like any Indian I'd ever seen.

I stuck my hand out. "I'm Dr. Green."

His calloused grip nearly crushed my knuckles.

"How long has he been like this?" I asked.

"'Bout a year." The chief took off his hat and lowered his head. "His time has come. I don't plan to take him home." He lifted his eyes and stared at me, waiting, it seemed, for my contradiction.

I nodded then ran my hand along his horse's swayed back and lifted the animal's tail. The undersurface was covered with clusters of the cancerous growths, most as big as grapes and smeared with ointment of garlic and God knows what else so thick I could almost taste it.

I sighed and wiped my greasy hands with a paper towel. The chief was right. The cancer had spread. Probably to the horse's intestines. Death would be slow and agonizing unless we intervened.

"What's your horse's name?" I asked while I stalled to collect my thoughts and formulate a plan.

"Whitehorse. He's been with me twenty-three years. We've gotten old together. He's got more heart than any horse I've ever known."

I swallowed. *Don't get too close. Makes the job too hard.*

I changed the subject. "What tribe are you from?" I asked, though I doubted he really had a drop of Indian blood in him with his pale skin and fine features.

"Narragansett."

Pretending I recognized the name, I raised my eyebrows. "My great-grandfather was Chickasaw."

Good Lord. Why on earth had I felt compelled to tell him that? I never knew my great-grandfather or if my family history was based on fact or just my mother's stories.

The old horse snorted and swung his head around. The chief nodded. "It's good, then, that we have come to you. Whitehorse tells me so."

A shiver rippled up my spine. Maybe it was fatigue, or perhaps it was the blast of winter wind from the breezeway that sent a chill over the room. Whitehorse looked at me, his eyes gentle and bemused.

To my relief my beeper buzzed. Insistent.

"Let me get this." I spun around and spoke across my shoulder while I reached for the phone. "You can take him to stall thirty."

The chief patted his horse on the neck. "He wants to know how you'll do it. And what will you do with him after?"

I started to answer, then halted. *Who wants to know? The horse?*

I cleared my throat and made sure I looked at the chief as I spoke. "I'll give him a shot. He'll lie down and go to sleep. We'll take the carcass to the incinerator. Would you like the ashes?"

Odd. I felt uneasy talking about this in front of the horse. In front of *this* horse.

The chief whispered into Whitehorse's ear. The old beast blinked and lowered his head.

"No. Don't want the ashes. Once the spirit leaves, the body is just dust. But I want to stay with him a while before you do it. Would that be okay?"

My heart squeezed. Ordinarily I would get this over with. There were other cases needing my attention before I went home. But somehow, telling the chief we had to do this immediately just didn't seem right.

I opened the gate to the stocks. "Sure. I'll check on a couple of other horses."

The old horse, lead rope tossed over his neck, followed the chief out of the exam room.

The sound of plodding hoof steps, tired and hollow, echoed down the barn.

"Dr. Green, that old Indian guy is still in his horse's stall. He's been chanting. It's kinda weird." A veterinary student in blue coveralls shoved her hands in her pockets. She had Whitehorse's medical record tucked underneath her arm. Dark circles rimmed her eyes and her shoulders drooped. "After we put the horse down, we're done, right? I need to get home and let my dogs out."

I glanced at my watch. Jeez, it was already nine o'clock at night. I felt like a walking zombie, numbed and anesthetized by exhaustion. But compared to my student, I figured I was used to it, conditioned by six long years of working in an equine emergency hospital.

Convinced I had the stamina of a racehorse and an outer skin as tough as horsehide, I took the record from the student. "I'll take care of this. Go home and get some rest."

She smiled, the gratefulness in her eyes unmistakable.

I headed toward stall number thirty with my heart as heavy as my footsteps.

The barn was calm this time of night. The soft sounds of horses eating, coughing, and shifting were the only noises.

Steam wafted from the hot bran mash that sat untouched in Whitehorse's bucket. The chief sat cross-legged in the corner of the stall. In his deep and trancelike voice, he sang a melancholy tune that I didn't recognize.

Whitehorse had his eyes closed, his head hung low. The sweat behind his ears and the way his nostrils flared indicated he was in pain. The two doses of analgesic I'd given him earlier had done little to ease his discomfort.

The chief rose and dusted the woodchip bedding off his jeans. "I'm leaving. Whitehorse and I have said our good-byes."

Vaguely ill at ease, I shifted and glanced at the windows above us. Snow streamed down from the night sky, the flakes as big as butterflies. The barn, though unheated, suddenly felt warm, and the sweet smell of last summer's hay reminded me of easier days with warm sun and languid afternoons watching horses graze while I took a break and ate my lunch.

The chief's eyes followed my gaze, looking upward. "Thank you, Dr. Green," he said softly.

The lump in my throat suddenly got too big to swallow. He was thanking me for putting down his horse?

I hesitated. "Chief, do you want to take his halter?"

Slipping the cherry red halter from his horse's head, the chief whispered in the animal's ear. He patted his horse on the neck, then stepped outside the stall. "Whitehorse says it is a good day to die. That was an old Indian saying before Hollywood made it famous. You ever heard it, Dr. Green?"

I nodded. *Could this guy be for real?*

The chief shook my hand. Without another word, he left. The sounds of his footsteps were almost imperceptible, his back straight and regal. If I had not seen his boots and hat, I would have sworn he had on moccasins and a feather headdress.

I grabbed a hospital halter, then rolled the stall door open. "Whitehorse, it's time," I said in a choked whisper. Nowadays, I rarely spoke out loud to the horses unless it was to say, "Whoa."

I led Whitehorse toward the breezeway into a wide, safe space.

As we trod down the aisle, the other horses hung their heads over their stall gates and watched us. A butter-colored Percheron, a draft horse with a head as big as an elephant's, knocked his chin against the door, banging, it seemed, a sort of salute.

As I pulled the syringe from my pocket, Whitehorse looked at me and raised his head. His eyes focused on the moon, which had suddenly appeared from behind the clouds and shimmered through the window.

"No more pain, Whitehorse. I promise." I slipped the needle into his jugular vein.

The great horse lowered his haunches, then came to rest on his side and laid down his head. He drew his last, ragged breath and closed his eyes, his ghostly white form awash in the soft glow of moonlight.

I could almost feel his spirit, hear his brave heart beating, and then fading away. The soul of Whitehorse, shadowy and whispering, swirled around me, then vanished.

My breath hitched. My heart skipped a beat. I stood there for a moment, confused and unnerved. How had this old horse gotten to me, set himself apart?

I closed my eyes.

Putting a horse down was a necessary part of my job. It was best to stay clinical, detached. Do it humanely and don't think about it. I'd taught myself to be unmoved, indifferent to the life force, if there was such a thing, as it left an animal's body.

But tonight I'd seen it. Felt it. I knew the heart of Whitehorse.

I'd been a veterinarian for eight years, and I had never before encountered such a passing.

Had I not been listening? Not watching?

And then it happened.

The horses in the barn began to whinny — the sick and ailing, the feeble newborns, and those ready to go home. Each one barely waiting for the last to finish. Minutes passed before their chorus ceased.

The hair on the back of my neck prickled. I opened my eyes, and suddenly a warm rush spread over me, washing away the cold, the fear, and most of all, the guilt.

It was always hard to take a life. And I realized now what was making me tired. No. Not tired. Burned out. How could I keep doing this?

The barn grew still; the horses settled. I took a deep breath, fighting back the urge to bolt, to go running from the barn, sobbing. I'd had enough.

My beeper wailed, puncturing the silence.

I held the phone in my shaking hand. Unable to respond, unwilling to start it all again, I slumped against the wall and stared at the cancer-ravaged body at my feet.

Whitehorse looked like he was sleeping. The creases at the corners of his mouth relaxed. His eyes were closed as if he rested in green grass and the summer sun.

Inexplicably, a languid sense of peace, of thankfulness and restoration, rose up from my heart.

I knew then why Whitehorse had come to me.

I held the phone to my ear. "Okay," I answered. "Tell Dr. Fitch I'll be here."

Meditation

Is there a horse who reminds you of the joy and meaning you used to find by giving service?

How to Embarrass a Horse

Duane Isaacson
Cutten, California

I rode my first horse at the age of forty-four. After overcoming my initial terror of these large animals, I acquired a horse for my daughters and one for myself. A horsewoman I knew suggested that I might be interested in natural horsemanship as a way to improve my relationship with horses.

With a manic obsession, I dived into learning the practices of natural horsemanship. I learned to work with my horse using his own language. I helped him feel safe being touched everywhere on his body and to get comfortable with strange things like plastic bags and feed sacks flopping around him. Together we gained control of his feet by moving his body until the two of us could dance around each other entirely free and at liberty.

When I saw how well these things worked and how easy they seemed to be, my ego got inflated. I began to fancy myself a horse trainer or perhaps even a horse whisperer. I was ready to tackle just about any difficult horse, so I purchased a horse at auction. He was a stocky, dark bay quarter horse about 15 hands tall. He had no white markings anywhere except for a small white spot near his withers where he'd been scarred by a saddle. Buck was being sold because he bucked off everyone who tried to ride him. If anyone merely tried to pet him, he'd pin back his ears and bite or kick.

And here I was with a big head and just enough knowledge to be dangerous.

Blissfully ignorant, I took on the challenge of training Buck. For two years he and I struggled to become friends, as I suffered painful bruises and sudden involuntary dismounts. Buck made major changes in how he viewed the world, largely in spite of me. He came

Duane and Buck

to understand that I wasn't about to hurt him, that his confusion and fear didn't trouble me, and that I would not add insult to injury by beating him for having emotions. He learned to carry a saddle and me, even though I rode like a sack of potatoes and frequently threw us both off balance. My own development was lagging behind. Buck was a far better student than I.

After months of work, I was still convinced that there was something I needed to fix about my horse, not something I needed to change within me. Whenever I lost sight of the importance of our relationship and got all wrapped up in myself, Buck would live up to his name. I'd hit the dirt. Hard. The breath knocked out of me, I'd spend several minutes on my hands and knees, gasping for air. There always seemed to be witnesses around who would offer help, but their presence only caused me intolerable embarrassment.

Three years went by, and our riding was going better. When they did occur, the bucking incidents had become rare and halfhearted. During those years I also began studying animal communication. I kept an open mind and tried to verify the communications I thought I received from Buck, but I was never quite sure of them. Nevertheless, there were some communications I found extremely difficult to chalk up to coincidence. One such incident occurred in front of a crowd of spectators.

Because of my success with calming Buck and some of the attention I received, I was invited to give a demonstration at a local training clinic. The clinic featured several trainers showing off their accomplishments and flashing their egos like strutting peacocks. I joined in the parading.

I had, on several occasions, bragged about my success with Buck. I became good at telling the story of how no one had been able to ride him until I came along — and on and on, ad nauseam. The clinic would be one more opportunity for me to display my incredible talents. I am surprised that on the day of the clinic, I could fit a hat on my swollen head.

I brought Buck into the round pen in front of about sixty people and proceeded to do a demonstration. We moved around in a quiet little dance while I talked to the crowd. At one point I received the clearest communication from Buck. It arrived in my heart as a feeling of embarrassment and in my head as the words: *Please don't tell them how I used to be.*

I was momentarily stunned as Buck managed to break through all my defenses against hearing what he had to say.

Buck had already overcome his past issues, with little help from me. It was no longer necessary that I keep repeating the story of his checkered past. In fact, glorifying myself was the only reason to continue talking about it.

So, what did I do?

In my infinite wisdom I ignored what Buck communicated and repeated the whole story to the crowd. I wanted admiration and applause. I bragged about being the only one who could handle this dangerous, incorrigible horse.

When I turned to look at Buck, after I finished spouting off, I was shaken to the core. I could almost see the tears in his eyes and the embarrassment on his face. I had stripped him naked in front of everyone.

Stuffing my guilty feelings and squelching the pain in my heart, I climbed in the saddle.

Over the years of our riding together I had finally learned that if I ignored Buck's attempts to communicate with me, he would simply try harder. He'd start with a whisper, then a shout, and when all else failed, he'd finally resort to bucking. Now, I had ignored his subtle communication. Knowing that I wasn't listening to him, he resorted to the only thing he knew that would get through to me. He started bucking. In front of everyone.

Thankfully, he was far more benevolent than I. He stopped just short of dumping me on the ground. I hung off the side of the saddle and felt the blood rise to my cheeks. Suddenly everything became clear, and it was my turn to be embarrassed at how I had humiliated him.

Later the same day, the point was driven home when I asked a professional animal communicator to talk to Buck about what had happened. Without any prompting from me, she said, "He was horribly embarrassed when you told all those people about his past after he asked you not to."

I lived most of my life not realizing I could embarrass my four-legged friends. I hadn't been aware that my horse was capable of such feelings until I embarrassed both of us. I will carry this story with me always. It serves as a pinprick to keep my ego deflated. And that makes my hat fit better.

Meditation

Has a horse helped you shrink your hat size? What did you learn about yourself and the horse?

Miracles Are Something to Believe In

Alexandra Best Flood
Sandwich, Massachusetts

*T*o be completely honest, Lilly, the pinto pony mare with a tan and white coat, whom I leased, is an angel. No questions asked. If you don't believe in miracles, here's a story for you.

I started riding at Percival Lane Farm in Sandwich, Massachusetts, in November of 2004 when I was ten, and now I am twelve. I had competed with Lilly in several shows and was looking forward to attending the Pinto World Show in Oklahoma in June 2005. This is a championship for all riders who show pinto horses and ponies. The show contains many different riding disciplines, with the most common being western, English, saddle seat, and dressage.

Two days before I was scheduled to leave for the Pinto World Show, Lilly reared up and fell on top of me. This horse is bombproof, so it was a complete fluke. My trainer, Jess, said that my accident was the worst she had ever experienced.

But I love Lilly even more now because when she fell on me, it saved my life.

After the accident I was taken to the hospital emergency room and given a bunch of tests, including a CAT scan. The tests showed that I had no broken bones but some internal bleeding. This, however, was the good news. The bad news was that the doctors had spotted something bad on the CAT scan. An aneurysm was stuck on the middle of my aorta, where my legs split. None of my doctors had ever seen an aneurysm in this location. The doctors believe that I was born with this condition. It was not caused by the fall.

The doctors at Children's Hospital in Boston were outstanding. They did surgery to remove the aneurysm. The surgery lasted almost seven hours. The doctors said that if it hadn't been taken out, I would have eventually died.

The week I was recovering in the hospital from the accident on Cape Cod, my trainer, Jess, was on her way to the Pinto World Show. Jess called me during every stop to see how I was and to tell me how Lilly was doing. At the show Lilly won Top 5 in showmanship and Top 10 in in-hand trail. I was psyched!

I had a feeling that my mom's friend, Darby, who died young, was my angel all along as well as Lilly. Darby used to ride and train horses. Every horse show I went to, my mom would tell me to pray to Darby for good luck. At one show I got all blue ribbons and won champion.

Alexandra and Lilly

After my surgery all I wanted to do was to see Lilly again. She was all I could think about. When I recovered I went straight to the barn. I couldn't help myself. As soon as I got there I saw that Lilly's mane was braided and fancy from being in the show. It looked like she had lost weight too.

I ran into her paddock and gave Lilly a hug, a kiss, and treats as I cried into her neck. I had missed her and needed to see that angelic pony once more. Tears welled up in my eyes as I thought more and more about the accident. I wasn't mad at her. I was greatly appreciative of the experience she gave me.

Yes, it was a very bad first fall. Yes, it was also a great first fall because it saved me.

I could not ride for over four months. As soon as I got back in the saddle, I went right to work. After a little bit I gained my full strength back and rode as well as I always did.

So maybe this story helped you to believe that miracles aren't just in dreams. They happen. Maybe it taught you to not frown or stick out your tongue but to try to find that halo on top of your horse's head, because all horses have them.

This experience taught me that you must give everything you have to be strong. You have to give everything to be who you are.

That's why Lilly is not just *some* pony, she's *the* pony who saved my life. Lilly has been and always will be the pony of my dreams and my angelic friend.

Meditation

What crises have come about that led to your better health?
Has a horse been the divine messenger for your healing?

Big Walter the Mule Led
Our Family to Alternative Healing

Leslie Robinson
Trenton, Florida

*M*y husband, Ric, and I were at a farm helping a veterinarian treat a large pig. When we walked through the barn, Walter the mule stuck his head over the top of a high stall wall to look at us. After we walked over to his stall door, he immediately stuck his head out to greet us. He seemed to enjoy being petted, even though we were strangers. We started to walk away from him, and he leaned even farther out of his stall, looking for more attention.

I could see that Walter was an outgoing, friendly fellow who had enjoyed our meet-and-greet. I asked his owner if the mule was for sale. I really hadn't planned to buy another equine, but the question just came out. She said no.

After we finished the pig work, I gave Walter, still hanging his head out of the stall door, one last glance, and we went home. Walter had said his bold hello, and then we were gone from his life. Or so it appeared.

About six months after we first met Walter, I got a call from his owner asking if we would be interested in buying him, as he was "just too big a mule." We talked it over and reluctantly went to look. I had never forgotten how Walter poked his big head over the stall wall to check us out. He was so interested in us. It seemed, upon later reflection, that Walter was meant to be part of our family from the first day we met him. We knew little about mules, but the thought of owning one intrigued us. He was a big, gangly guy, yet his size never concerned us. It was almost as if those details didn't matter. We decided to buy him with no veterinarian check and after being given only a minimal history.

Walter was supposed to be five years old, but he was in his fourth home because of this problem people had with his being too big. Mules are pushy by nature and very intelligent. They want to get their way or at least to think they got their way. A large, assertive mule can be a handful. Walter did, indeed, seem a bit pushy to us, even though we didn't know much about mules.

Leslie and Walter

We commented to the owner that Walter had sores on his forelegs. Later these would be sites where tumors appeared. The seller said that the sores were caused by rough play, and we took her word for all of it.

As months passed the sores grew larger. Walter also developed some really nasty dermatitis on his shoulders, with terrible itching. He outgrew several halters. We decided to take him to a holistic vet for an opinion about his serious skin condition. Among other things, the vet believed that Walter had cancer. She diagnosed Walter's condition with a thorough physical exam, physical and mental history, pulse diagnosis, chiropractic assessment, and homeopathic workup. She said that his age was only eighteen months to one year. This meant he had much more growing to do. She began treating him, and we were off on a healing journey.

Meanwhile, we were reading everything we could find about mule care and mule training and thought we were prepared for dealing with a mule. Unfortunately, we made our share of mistakes.

I tried to use the techniques of several horse clinicians to establish a relationship with Walter. An equine's response to the application of pressure to a body part or lead rope is very important for safe performance. This is especially true with a mule, since mules have to *want* to do what a person asks. In fact, if a person can make the mule think it was the mule's original idea, so much the better. Mules enjoy outsmarting people whenever the people aren't performing up to the mules' standards.

One day I asked Walter to come along with me by giving him a pull on his lead rope. Instead of moving forward to my cue, he stopped in his tracks, contemplated doing what I had asked, and then said no. He turned and ran away, pulling the rope out of my hands and taking some of my skin along with it. To this day, he will still pull away when I ask him to do something he doesn't want to do. For example, he likes going to the vet's office, so when it's time to go home he won't get on the trailer. This is why I don't ride him. I feel that what he does with a halter on, he may also do under saddle. When a mule pulls away all of the time, it basically makes him undesirable as a saddle mule.

Walter continued to grow to his current approximate weight of 1,500 pounds and height of 17 hands. What a big guy he is! Because of his size, when Walter says no, it means no. There is no holding him when he wants to run away. However, he is very gentle, kind, and charming. He loves contact with people, especially when it includes a good ear scratch.

We continued our holistic treatments with minimal success but remained sure that Western medicine was not the way to go. I was sure that a more traditionally oriented vet would want to surgically remove Walter's tumors or suppress his dermatitis with topical medicines, which could cause even more illness.

Walter's illness brought us together with a holistic vet who is a skilled healer and teacher. Almost without hesitation, I started taking her three-year class on holistic therapies for equines. I have learned about the Eastern philosophies of medicine, including acupuncture, herbal therapy, and homeopathy, and I will soon be studying bodywork.

Since I am a registered nurse and have practiced Western medicine for over thirty years, I am enjoying learning another approach to health. Already my husband and I have changed health practices for our entire animal family and ourselves. We also now understand the importance of a natural healthy diet for all of us and how emotional health affects our well-being.

It is almost as if Walter had a mission to put us on the path toward healthier living that is right for us. We recently moved to a beautiful rural area of Florida. As a result of the new environment and continued holistic vet care, Walter's health has improved. In our previous location we were subjected to a lot of emotional stress, which affected our animals, particularly Walter. Our life was unsettled, and Walter seemed to know it. He was more withdrawn from us and the other animals. His skin condition was severe, and his tumors grew larger.

Since the move, Walter's tumors have reduced in size, and he has little to no itching. In several places the tumors have been replaced with normal-appearing tissue and his health has greatly improved. In our new home he is flourishing. He keeps watch on the forty acres we share with the neighbors and their horses. He notices all comings and goings of cars, cats, dogs, and goats. Even his pulling-away behavior has reduced in frequency, and he is more willing to do what is asked of him.

Walter will always be part of our family, despite our difficulties. I thank God that Walter stuck his head out of the stall that fall day to say hello.

Meditation

Are you looking at the health alternatives and options for healing a horse or yourself?

Shetland Pony Shaggy's Healing Journey

Steve Schwertfeger
Crystal Lake, Illinois

*T*he phone rang on a cold Sunday morning in Crystal Lake, Illinois. When I answered it, I heard a clearly upset voice on the other end. Donna Ewing from the Hooved Animal Rescue and Protection Society explained to me that a real estate agent had reported a very urgent situation. She had seen what looked to her like an abused horse at a farm. Since I am a state-licensed volunteer humane investigator for our organization, Donna needed my help.

Within the hour, we were barreling down the highway, trying to prepare ourselves emotionally for what might lay ahead. Would we find an animal horribly suffering or near death, or would this report be just a false alarm?

We arrived at the address of a farm that was for sale. As state-licensed investigators, we have the right to enter the barn, but sometimes it can be less stressful and confusing if the owner comes along with us. So we knocked several times on the front door of the house until we concluded that nobody was home.

We went to the freezing barn and immediately found a dead horse lying in a stall, obviously starved. The poor creature was very thin and covered in large ulcers from lying down for a long period of time. I cannot begin to explain the feeling of cold, empty sadness that overtook me. The poor animal had experienced a long, painful death. I wondered how anyone with a conscience could have allowed this to happen.

After checking over the horse, we took pictures to send to the Department of Agriculture. Photos are a state requirement to assist in any legal action that may be taken against the owner and to serve as backup to our claims about what we observed. While doing the photos, we heard a muffled, scraping noise coming from the back of the barn. Since there was no electricity in the dark barn, we focused our flashlights toward the sound, expecting to see a raccoon or a stray cat. The light illuminated a Shetland pony who was chained to the wall. Donna and I looked at each other apprehensively.

We saw that the pony's hooves were horribly overgrown. His brown coat was ragged looking. His stomach was distended. We removed the chain and helped him hobble into the light cast from the open door. He was disoriented and had a very difficult time. At this point my sadness and repressed anger were replaced with a somewhat confusing sense of relief. Our arrival at the barn that day perhaps would still save a life.

We called the Department of Agriculture and got permission to have the pony removed from the premises and taken to our farm, owned by the Hooved Animal Rescue and Protection Society. There a veterinarian and a farrier examined the pony. The good news was that the pony's physical condition was curable with several types of medicine, plenty of water, and good quality food. His feet were another matter.

Since the hooves were overgrown to the point of curling upward, a condition known as Turkish slippers, the bones in his feet were starting to adjust to this abnormal growth. The farrier decided to trim the feet slowly, allowing the bones to readjust so that in time the pony could again walk normally.

During his several months of treatment, the pony, whom we named Shaggy, very slowly regained the ability to walk. His physical condition continued to improve. In the middle of the summer that year, a local classroom of children came to the farm to visit the animals.

During their visit Shaggy came alive. He loved all the attention. He pranced around as if he wanted to let the children know how well he was feeling, absorbing all of their attention. The kids, in turn, reflected Shaggy's joyfulness back to him. They loved brushing, petting, feeding, and talking to him.

Shaggy with little friend, Natalie Hinz

After that day, several local schools called to ask if Shaggy could visit their preschoolers. Each time we made the decision to transport Shaggy only after evaluating his daily condition and assessing how he would react to the attention. We would make sure that no new problems had occurred to impede the progress he had made in regaining his health. Before Shaggy made any trip we checked that he was eating, drinking, and walking well.

Now, whenever Shaggy walks off the trailer to make a school visit, he becomes like a movie star prancing down the red carpet. He wallows in the attention from the preschoolers and seems very happy to allow the young children to experience his regal presence. Since the children we visit are so young, we have to tell Shaggy's story with restraint, and they are always moved by it. When he interacts with the children, his upbeat personality overcomes their concerns about his rough start in life. One school even organized a class fund-raiser so the children could assist with Shaggy's care and receive updates on how he is doing and what his current antics might be.

When I look at pictures of Shaggy and his adoring visitors, I smile and dwell on the healing journey of this animal, who was unwanted, alone, cold, chained to a wall, and staring uncomprehendingly into the unchanging darkness. And then I think of the beneficent providence that decreed he would be whisked suddenly into a new existence of good food, companionship, movement, and people who care for him. I don't believe that any abused pony had a better life after being rescued.

Sometimes, when we are alone, Shaggy walks up to me. He looks at me thoughtfully, and I get the impression that he is somehow, in his own way, thanking me.

Meditation

How could you overcome rough starts and find ways to give fulfilling service?

Our Angel in a Horse Coat

Sheryl Jordan
Grantsville, Maryland

Every day as I drove to work, I would slow down at a field that I passed and look at the herd of rough, unkempt ponies. One pony in particular caught my eye. He was young, with a reddish brown coat, short back, and long legs. He had a beautiful face and a long, flowing silver-flaxen mane and tail. In addition to his physical attributes and excellent conformation, he had a beautiful presence about him and a spirit of freedom in the way he carried himself.

I was thinking about getting a pony for my daughter, who was nine years old at the time, so I went house to house until I located the owner of the ponies. I asked him what he bred the ponies for, and sadly, he said that he ran a stallion with a herd of mares and sold the offspring at the killer market. At that time he was getting more per pound for horse meat than for beef. "In fact," he said, "this group of young ponies is going to the sale in two weeks."

I asked to go into the field so I could take a closer look at the pony. When I did, he and another pony, his half brother, warily checked me out from a distance. I watched the reddish brown pony I had admired trot and loved his beautiful way of moving. When I asked the pony's price, the man said, "Three hundred dollars." I immediately wrote a check.

This man also told me that the ponies had never been handled or halter broke. Whenever he shipped his ponies, he herded them onto a stock trailer. My first thoughts were, *What have I done? I just bought a wild, unbroken pony for my daughter.* Even though I was a professional with horses, I knew this had not been a wise move. There was something about this pony, though. Intuitively I felt a sense of peace, as if there were a reason for my connection with him.

Several days later I took my daughter, Angela, to see the pony in the field. He was off in the distance with the herd, and it was difficult to see him. Angela climbed over the fence and started walking toward the herd. Suddenly the pony lifted his head from grazing, left the herd, and came running up to my daughter. She did not know if she should run or stay put. She froze, and as he got closer, she put her hand out to him. Incredibly he put his muzzle into her cupped hand as if to say, "I choose you."

This was the pony's first human contact, and he had chosen to initiate it. I got goose bumps on my body and tears in my eyes as I watched. How did he know that he was ours?

Angela and Sugar

As Angela walked back to me with an incredulous smile on her face, the pony followed her to the fence.

Several days later, somehow, they got a halter on him and the pony was delivered to our barn. I walked him to a stall. Although he had not been halter trained and even though he was excited, he followed me obediently. His eyes were wide with fright; his long mane tossed about as he shook his head. I wasn't worried about his adjustment. As unusual as it is for a wild horse to do, this pony had chosen to trust us immediately, so I knew there would be something special about our relationship with him.

Angela and I started working with him slowly, gaining his trust and getting him used to grooming, eating treats, and being handled. He learned incredibly quickly and seemed to love the attention. We named him Shadowood's Sugar Maple since he is the color of maple syrup.

I started Sugar's training in a round pen. It did not take long for him to make eye contact and then willingly follow me around as if we were partners in a dance. He willingly accepted the tack and having Angela riding upon his back. She did all of his training. One year later we started showing Sugar on our local circuit in walk-trot classes in both English and western tack. Sugar ended up being champion pony for the year. Angela and Sugar also enjoyed riding on the trails, although Sugar wasn't crazy about the deer and would spin when surprised. But that taught Angela to sit tight.

In the following years Angela and Sugar moved up to showing in the canter classes, then to showing over fences. Again Sugar became champion pony for each of those years. He easily won over the horses in the jumping classes. Someone once approached me and offered ten thousand dollars for Sugar, but I said, "No, he will never be for sale."

Sugar has taught my daughter faith, commitment, dedication,

and hard work. He has given a lifetime of beautiful memories to her and to me.

Sadly, by the time she turned fourteen, Angela had outgrown her first pony. But Sugar continues to be with us, teaching my young students how to ride, which he does with infinite patience. He is the favorite and will once again be involved in a season of showing.

Unknown to us, Sugar Maple had sired a few foals. When we purchased him he had been gelded. A friend of ours went to purchase a horse from the same guy we bought Sugar from, and he pointed out to her that one of the pony mares was Sugar's daughter. She had a handsome little colt by her side. Sadly, their destination was also the killer market. My friend contacted me, and I immediately purchased both mare and foal.

The mare was seven or eight years old, and she and her colt had never been handled. We named the mare Shadowood's Golden Aspen, since she is a palomino Appaloosa. We gave her colt the name Shadowood's Silver Willow. The colt is the same color as his grand-sire, Sugar Maple.

Sugar Maple is a gift from God in our lives and an answer to our prayers. Every day we are thankful that his cute and intelligent face greets us as we enter the barn. I thank God that we saved him from the killers. He repays us with his love, trust, and willingness to please. He is our angel in a horse coat.

Meditation

Has a rescued horse rescued you and given something precious in return?

Soul-Saver Horse

Chrissy K. McVay
Little Switzerland, North Carolina

*W*hen I was fifteen I went through the usual high school peer pressure and started to hang out with kids who preferred booze parties to studying. My grades did a cliff dive, and so did my attitude toward life. The only time I felt like my soul was alive was when I partied. I turned belligerent toward my parents, lied to them, and sneaked out of the house as often as possible at night. I attended secret parties in cornfields or abandoned houses scattered along country roads in our small farming community.

My mother recognized the symptoms of a troubled teen and realized I needed a strong distraction from the bad influences. She also knew that the power of love could teach responsibility and bolster self-worth far faster than any lectures from parents or counselors. I'd always had a tremendous adoration of animals and dreamed that one day I would own a horse. When my mother had the money, an opportunity to buy a young Arabian gelding named Renegade seemed a gift from heaven. I'd just turned sixteen. My mother's birthday gift to me would change my life forever.

People cautioned my mother that buying such a high-strung creature was crazy. Renegade had a wild streak and needed dedicated, gentle discipline, but so did I. My mother was wise enough to know I needed a special challenge far outside of myself. Focusing only on my own selfish desires was leading me down dangerous avenues.

I saw in Renegade not only his untamed spirit but also his fear of the unknown. Renegade was struggling with a deep uncertainty that often afflicts inexperienced youth. I didn't know how to reassure him but believed that we could get through the uncertainty together. I wanted him to trust me, and I had to be worthy of that trust by making more mature choices.

I was immediately consumed with tutoring my bay gelding. He had a beautiful white crescent on his fiery brown forehead and a black mane and socks. I kept his burgundy-colored coat well groomed. The neighbors teased me that he was so shiny, he blinded them when they drove down the road. I barely thought of anything other than taking care of Renegade. I no longer had time for surly boozers, and they quickly lost interest in "that horse girl."

As soon as my homework was finished in the evenings, I rode Renegade. We joined a local 4-H Club and spent our weekends either practicing or at horse shows. I met new friends who had positive goals in life, and they urged me on as I pursued my own.

Renegade and I learned about discipline together. At first, partly out of fear and stubbornness, he refused to do simple things like backing up, crossing a shallow mud puddle, or getting into a trailer. It took patience and constant reassurance, but I soon taught him that I wasn't there just to show my authority. I wanted to help him get past these obstacles. Eventually he seemed to see how easy my requests were and started responding to my voice and gentle commands with confidence and without hesitation.

The melancholy person I'd been before seemed so far behind me that I never once looked back at that downward lifestyle until

Chrissy and Renegade

I was an adult and Renegade had died. At the time of his death he was twenty-nine years old and enjoying retirement at a nice boarding stable with another Arabian gelding named Rajah. Renegade died two weeks after his friend Rajah's death and two weeks before Christmas.

I knew a broken heart had caused Renegade's heart attack. Rajah was about the same age as Renegade and had been his friend for nearly ten years. They were the only two horses still boarded in a huge pasture. Renegade and Rajah seldom wandered very far from each other, even when grazing.

Losing my special friend, Renegade, left me with a broken heart too, but I was grateful for how he'd helped me through my adolescent struggles. I cringe sometimes when I ponder what direction my life might have taken if Renegade hadn't come along when he did. He was so much more than an undisciplined, spirited horse. Renegade was a true soul saver.

Meditation

How has a horse been a divine messenger to help you get back onto a healthier course and to make better choices?

Listening to Horses

Lynn Baskfield
Minneapolis, Minnesota

*H*orses are intuitive beings who can, in an instant, show people when they are fooling themselves or are on the right track. As herd animals, tuned in to the slightest inconsistency in their environments, horses mirror back to people the thoughts or feelings that people are not aware of. Horses can become healers and teachers by helping people deepen into their own authentic spirits after identifying behaviors that keep them from moving forward in life.

Horses provide wonderful metaphors for dealing with challenging situations in people's lives. Horses reflect back exactly what a human's body language tells them. Their unflagging honesty makes them especially effective messengers. Horses are naturally able to respond to human thoughts and emotions in very specific and clear ways. This allows people who work with them to discover a unique path to accomplishing their most cherished goals.

Using the natural affinity between people and horses, my business partner, Ann Romberg, and I designed Wisdom Horse Coaching, LLC, an equine-guided life coaching service that allows our clients to gain insights that they can immediately apply to their lives. Ann and I are part of a growing field called equine-guided education

(EGE). It gives me great joy every day to witness the miracles that horses bring about. No matter what results people hope to achieve when they come to a coaching session, for almost everyone, horses touch them at a much deeper level than they expected. Sometimes they evoke a long-forgotten memory; sometimes they open a heart with their gentleness; sometimes they help clients face their deepest fears. Ninety-percent of our EGE activities are done on the ground, without the need for riding a horse, making it possible for clients, with or without horse experience, to benefit from the work.

EGE focuses on nonverbal communication, since that is how a horse speaks. The horse's body picks up what is congruent or incongruent in a person's body. Horses naturally use their bodies to know the world. Likewise, we encourage participants of our workshops to smell, touch, see, and hear the horses.

The emphasis on nonverbal communication is one reason that our form of EGE is so effective. Although at this time in history we humans rely heavily on language, we are still wired, as our ancestors were, to learn things through our bodies. The body first picks up things that can be described in language only later — seeing a shadow in the alley and sensing danger, feeling the wind on your face and realizing that a storm is coming, or observing a child's body language and knowing something is wrong. Humans today have learned to distrust the body's knowingness and to rely on language to articulate what the body is directly observing and feeling. Relying on cognitive thinking means that people often override their intuitive body-mind response.

Working with horses, who rely upon their intuitive natures and their bodies instead of human language, taps in to a person's cellular memory. Dr. Candace Pert, professor of physiology and biophysics at Georgetown University Medical School and leading researcher in the field of body-mind science, speaks of the "wisdom of the body" and believes that the mind and emotions are present in each cell of the body.[6] As Ann and I practice EGE, we find that when activated, cellular memory reveals patterns and beliefs that might be different from what a person says or thinks. When buried belief patterns come to light, our clients gain access to whole new ways of becoming truer to themselves.

We design activities to simulate and reflect emotions and thought patterns that come up in our clients' daily lives. A person who has trouble saying no, for example, learns to notice how much discomfort he will put up with before he sets a limit for a horse who pushes at him with his nose. The first nudging might seem cute, or the client may feel he is getting special attention, but if he doesn't set a clear limit, the horse will become more insistent. The client will *have to* do something. What he does with the horse — back away, get confused, become aggressive, make nice — is exactly what he does in life when his boundaries are breached.

We don't try to direct our clients' experiences or predict the outcomes. Instead, we let horses and people have their natural interactions. This allows our clients to creatively solve problems by experimenting and making new choices. Equine-guided life coaches and educators listen to both horse and human. By employing skills of observation, curiosity, open-ended questioning, and intuition, they bridge the horse-human connection. Ann and I keep our verbal presentations to a minimum and completely trust the horses to guide the learning. We often take people out in the pasture, where the horses choose with whom they will work on a given day. Most horses are eager to step in and go to work. Clients go home with renewed confidence in themselves and new ways to relate to their loved ones and business associates.

The Horses Accept a New Member of Their Herd

As Joe, a fifty-two-year-old entrepreneur, ambled with Ann and me through a pasture of fifty horses, a couple of the horses gave Joe curious sniffs and then went back to grazing. On the way up a hill, Joe stopped and asked, "Did I mention that I'm afraid of horses?"

His question explained why it had taken him so long to accept our invitation to visit with the horses. We told him all that horses want from a person is honesty. We looked around at the magnificent herd and asked Joe, "Who is your herd?"

"I've never felt part of the herd," he replied.

Even though he worked with people every day, Joe felt separate. He remembered being left out of sports teams and not being invited to social events. He decided early on in his life that he didn't need to belong to groups.

As we wandered to the top of the hill, a horse named Cupid purposefully sauntered over to join us. As if at a cocktail party, we all stood in a little conversation cluster with Cupid to Joe's left and Ann and I to his right. Although I don't remember what we talked about, Cupid listened as though waiting for his chance to enter the conversation.

We noticed his attentiveness and started to walk again through the herd. Cupid followed us. When we stopped walking, Cupid stood at Joe's side. Only now he placed himself between Joe and us as if laying claim to him. We moved again to another part of the pasture, and Cupid walked right along with us.

"Maybe he likes me," Joe said. "That's cool, but I'm still afraid of horses."

Joe stroked Cupid on the shoulder but didn't want him any closer. As Cupid leaned into his touch, it occurred to Joe that this horse *really* liked him. Another horse came over for a sniff. Cupid laid his ears back and chased her off. Whether he'd volunteered to form a team with Cupid or not, within another few minutes Joe had clearly been chosen by the horse. "I can't get this guy to go away." Joe said.

Standing out in the pasture with Cupid, who was now nuzzling the shirt buttons over Joe's heart, Joe said that he knew about guardian angels, but they had never felt real. "Now I know what it is to have a guardian angel," he said with a crack in his voice. A horse had accepted him in a way he had never been accepted by humans. He called later to say, "I get it finally. I'm actually part of the herd!"

Since that meeting with Cupid, Joe has become a contributing member of several "herds." He is on the staff of a local university and of two well-known organizations that mentor other professionals.

From Darkness, Light

In the Insights for Writers workshop that we teach as one of the offerings of the Loft Literary Center in Minneapolis, horses also help writers tell their stories — not necessarily the pretty ones, but the ones that need to be told.

We do an exercise in which we ask the participants to take turns standing with a horse in the center of the round pen and talk about what they are burning to write about. Once they get clear about their true desires, the writers lunge the horse as a metaphor for getting their story out onto the page and into the world.

Lunging is one of the many exercises we use to help clients see if what they are saying lines up with what really matters to them. Since horses read energy, if what a person declares before lunging is not clear or meaningful to her, the energy with which she extends herself in asking the horse to move will be inconsistent. The horse will pick that up and perform — or not perform — in ways that reflect back what is really going on.

Ann, Dude, and Lynn

It's important to note that EGE is not horsemanship. In EGE learning situations even people with extensive horse backgrounds cannot get horses to move consistently — or at all — if their declarations do not have clarity or meaning for them.

In one class several people worked with Desi, a lovely gray Arabian mare. Bev spoke about completing her travel memoirs. She spent some time describing the exciting adventures she had been on but had yet to write about. Even though Bev gave Desi what she thought was a signal to move around the pen, Desi stopped several times to rub her rear end against the fence. It looked as if Desi was in heat, but she wasn't. Further into the session, we learned that Bev was in a new, very passionate relationship. We all had to laugh at how accurately Desi had reflected the real truth: The writer wasn't writing — and hadn't been for a while — because she was having too much fun in the new relationship.

Another client, Patty, said that she wanted to write about midlife transition. She spoke about her subject in serious tones. Her shoulders rounded as she looked at the ground. No matter how much effort Patty made to get Desi moving, the horse would walk a couple of steps and stop. Desi would not move out toward the edge of the round pen, nor would she pay much attention to Patty. With a little coaching, Patty became aware of how heavily her chosen writing subject was weighing upon her. In all other areas of life, humor had been her strong suit. What would happen if she lightened up and put some humor into the idea of moving through midlife? When Patty had these thoughts, her body straightened as she brightened up. She made a joke, looked at Desi, and with very little physical effort had her trotting smoothly around the outside edge of the round pen.

After the first four people had lunged Desi, we retired her and brought George, a solidly built Appaloosa gelding, into the ring. One of the participants, Marie, had been sitting in her chair with her arms folded across her chest, observing the others. What could she learn from a horse? To her, what had taken place with the other writers looked like a lot of mumbo jumbo. But now it was her turn.

Standing in the round pen with George, Marie talked about love and a wedding. She spoke of singing birds and the beauty of nature. These are the things she said she was burning to write about. But her body was rigid. Her eyes were strained. Her energy was tentative and contracted. As she spoke of lovely things, George, standing in front of her and looking her square in the eye, took a big pee. Then Desi, who was still in the larger arena, being held by an assistant, also took a pee.

Now, often a horse peeing is just that and nothing more. But horses won't hold on to energy that wants to be discharged. They respond with their bodies to a person who is holding on to a stressful situation: they may roll on the ground or shake themselves off, and sometimes they pee.

Observing both George and Desi pee after they heard Marie say the lovely things she wanted to write about, I asked, "Marie, what are you pissed about?"

Startled at this seemingly off-the-wall question, she hesitated. "I don't want to go there," she replied, looking at the ground. But the question had touched a place in her that was authentic, raw, and seemed to be ready to be revealed. "I know you don't want to go there and you don't have to talk about it out loud, but what you don't want to go to is the real stuff. Will you let yourself be with what is coming up for you?"

"Yes," she whispered.

Ann and I asked the others to hold a safe space for woman and horse. "Would you be willing," we asked Marie, "to just stand in the round pen with George and listen to him — with your heart?"

She nodded. In silence we held the space for several minutes while Marie and George looked into each other's eyes. Tears flowed quietly down Marie's cheeks.

That day we did not find out what Marie connected with. She needed time to let it all in. As the weeks went by, though, she began to share about the experience of being raped — something that she'd told herself she had already handled. She shared how it seemed such a coincidence that we chose a gelding for her to work with. She spoke of seeing in his eyes the possibility of healing and maybe even of healing others. And she knew she couldn't tell the stories of light, which she so wanted to tell, without also writing her story of terror and darkness from the rape.

As Marie began to share with the other class participants, another woman told us that she too had been raped. We had conversations about healing, empowerment of women, and speaking our truth. Marie wrote an extraordinary piece that brought us into the heart of her experience and made all of us think about what a raped woman feels beyond anything revealed by a headline in the newspaper. When people listen to the wisdom of the horses and honor their ways of knowing, miracles of transformation happen.

Meditation

When have horses mirrored back to you an attitude or emotion that you have hidden from yourself?

Smooth as Silk

Holly Leigh
Ipswich, Massachusetts

After a severe hand injury, I lost all finger dexterity as well as all sensitivity to textures and to hot and cold. When I first returned to riding horses after fifteen years away, I questioned whether I could reclaim much independence. It would be impossible for me to pick feet, to fasten the noseband buckle, or secure the even smaller throatlatch.

I learned how to make minor adjustments. I attach shoelace loops to zip and unzip my paddock boots, but I need assistance with my half-chaps, spurs, and helmet chinstrap. Someone must hold my wrist offside when I mount. I knot the reins so my wrist fits into the V end.

Once onboard a horse called Silky, I find a missing rhythm. We are partners for an hour once or twice a week. Though small in stature, Smooth As Silk is aptly named for her dainty stride, her perfect upward flying changes.

"She has the prettiest canter," sighs Robin, who owns Silky and is my trainer.

A small chestnut mare with a splash of white on her forehead, Silky reminds me of those hard caramel candies with the white nougat center. In spring her coat blooms with dapples that last until fall. At age twenty-three, she still acts feisty. She paws her shavings, nickers, and rolls the white rims of her eyes to make her carrot and apple desires known.

Silky has a great work ethic and with enthusiasm muscles us over fences with her ears pricked. Throughout the jumping course, a sea theme decorates the various apparatuses. Cutouts of seahorses and shells mark the standards, buoys hang on a gate jump, and lighthouses bracket the roll-top. In a pattern of S-turns and lead changes, we travel together over the green box, the planks painted with waves, the white gate, an oxer, and assorted cross rails.

Riding again allows me to immerse myself in the changes in seasons, how the horses' coats respond, how the New England woods promise color. Plastic pumpkins and real gourds appear under the rails. And though I lose my reins sometimes in a heart-stopping way when I jump, I would not trade the fluent feel of Silky when she bows her back over an obstacle, when she folds and floats like a feather that rises under me.

Coming upon age forty, I feel drawn now to the coastal zone where land and sea both clash and merge, where I can allow the slow erosion of cares. During the winter we often trailer the horses five minutes over to the beach to ride at low tide. The dunes look lunar in their whiteness, and whitecaps flare beyond the sandbars. We bundle against the wind in bulky layers.

On my initiation to the beach on horseback, I saw a man riding his horse in the rippling water's edge and walking his dog on a very long leash. Robin told me about a woman who rides in the winter, bareback, in a wetsuit.

Today, overhead, a faint sun disc shines and illuminates rivulets that vein the wet, packed sand. I listen to Silky's nostrils flutter as we walk away from the wind. About a mile down the beach we trot; at two miles we canter. The hoofbeats sound as audible as heartbeats. I am surprised how hollow the hooves sound when striking wet sand, like rattling coconuts or castanets, like drums. As Silky accelerates past the others, her blue wool quarter-sheet flapping, I cede any notion of control and surrender to her speed. I concentrate on our shadow running alongside us.

I am gasping by the time I pull Silky up. We face the incoming waves as we wait for the others to reach us. I pant with the exhilaration and relief of surviving a fast ride. The other horses walk and splash in the rippling sheets of water, but Silky prefers to keep her feet dry.

Later we cross the dunes to the parking lot, and the horses sink as they sashay down in what feels like sand pillows. Thanks to Silky, I am able to push my boundaries. I once again feel a part of the physical world.

Meditation

When do horses reconnect you with nature and the physical world? How could you better nurture this connection and yourself?

Ask Zeke

Dear Zeke,

Why are horses such good healers? My horse seems to always know exactly how I feel. If I'm sad, he makes me laugh. If I am sick, he makes me feel better. How does he do that?

Sincerely,
Perplexed

Dear Perplexed,

Since ancient times, horses have kissed Mother Earth with their hooves. At the same time, our heads thrust forward as we listen to the whispers of Sister Wind. Being at peace with the wind and in harmony with the earth connects horses with Nature's secret healing energies.

Creation and destruction are the two faces of healing. Horses know this to be true. We watch as Mother Earth grows new life and embraces the dead in her arms. We stand silently as Sister Wind blows away sadness and takes whatever has become precious.

Horses carry wisdom about healing in their hearts. We give it to any humans who have the humility to hear us. And we ask for very little in return.

Naturally yours,
Zeke

CHAPTER THREE

Courage and Endurance

Here lies Copenhagen
The charger ridden by the Duke of Wellington
the entire day
of the Battle of Waterloo
Born 1808, died 1836.
God's humbler instrument, though meaner clay,
Should share the glory of that glorious day.

— Epitaph on Copenhagen's tombstone

erhaps, of their many qualities, courage and endurance are the ones most admired in horses. Throughout history horses have carried soldiers into battle and stood their ground through the fiercest fights.

A leader riding into battle or in danger of being captured by the enemy was easier for the troops to see if he sat astride a white horse. Napoleon Bonaparte's favorite horse was the white stallion Marengo, whom Napoleon rode through both his Austrian victory and his Moscow retreat. Marengo's training consisted of tests such as having guns and cannons fired near him, having dogs and pigs run through his legs, and keeping a steady stride even when regiments and wagons came close. When Napoleon was exiled to Elba, he took Marengo. This is the horse he rode for his defeat at the Battle of Waterloo.

On the other side of the battlefield, the Iron Duke of Wellington rode the chestnut stallion Copenhagen, fighting for six years against Napoleon's troops. At the Battle of Waterloo he fought from early in the morning and throughout the entire day on the horse. In *Famous Horses and Their People*, historian and author Edna Hoffman Evans writes,

> At ten o'clock that night, after eighteen hours in the saddle, a weary Duke of Wellington dismounted in order to have a conference with the Prussian commander. The Iron Duke was bone tired, but not his horse. The chestnut still had energy enough to lash out hard with a final kick; there was so much power in his hoofs that if they had struck the Duke, they could have injured him severely. But fortunately they missed and who could blame him? All day bullets and cannon balls had roared and whistled around him, so wasn't he entitled to one last kick in the celebration?

When the horse died in 1836, the duke left London to give Copenhagen a burial with military honors at his estate.[1]

Today the courage of horses continues to be called upon by mounted police and forest rangers. Training for these horses includes learning to maneuver around stacks of burning hay and overcoming the tendency to shy at unexpected noise, gunshots, sirens, the clanging of heavy rocks against metal, and other frightening distractions.

Volunteers as well as sworn police officers ride these horses, who can often get to more places faster than a police car. These horses break up fights and burglaries in progress. On the more pleasant days they march in local parades.

In this chapter you will meet horses who have the courage, strength, and stamina that can and does save lives. They have so much heart that you will wonder how they can possibly be so brave. As for endurance, the horses in these stories weather every storm. They teach the people in their lives how to age gracefully. They greet life on their own terms while selflessly giving service to others.

The horses in this chapter are divine messengers who assure people that when all seems lost, they will not desert the ones they love or give up on the jobs they are committed to do.

Angel for a Day

Robert (Bob) Wagner
Neosho, Missouri

*S*ixty years ago I was growing up on a farm in eastern South Dakota. My dad wouldn't think of having an animal for a pet. His philosophy was that animals had to earn their keep. Cats provided rodent control. Dogs helped to drive and control other farm animals. Ponies rounded up and drove cattle or sheep and served as our transportation. It was only during our little bit of leisure time that Dad would permit me to have fun and ride the ponies for sport.

The two ponies I remember best were Cricket and Kayo. Cricket was lazy and easygoing. Kayo was always eager to finish our jobs. He seemed delighted to take off with a gallop when I tried to mount him. We would go the distance of two or three city blocks before I could gain full control of him.

In those days I rode the ponies bareback without saddles and usually guided them with reins on their bridles. But with or without bridles, the ponies would also go in the direction I leaned or would respond to a firm push on the neck. My two older brothers, who were taller and stronger, could mount the ponies by grabbing a bit of mane and slinging their legs over the horses' backs. But as a seventh grader, I was still too short to mount that way. I had to try to jump up with my stomach on Kayo's back so my head would be on one side and my legs on the other. Then I could swing one leg over his back and begin my journey.

During chore time my brothers did the heavy farm work. My job was to bring the cattle in from the pasture. I had to work Kayo for one week while Cricket was let out to pasture. The next week it would be Cricket's turn. I usually dreaded when it was Kayo's week to help with the job because he was so energetic and independent.

One night after school, a storm was coming. During my one-mile walk home, I bent into a fierce wind that blew snow at my face. It was getting dark, so I hurried to the barn. Since this week was Kayo's turn to bring in the cattle, I was afraid he would be even more difficult to mount because I wore heavy winter clothes.

I led Kayo out of the barn and jumped onto him. He galloped off, but I couldn't get my leg over him. I fell off. He immediately stopped and I tried again, without success. Then I led him over to the fence post. Using the woven fence wire as a ladder, I hoisted myself onto the horse.

The snow was already getting deeper, but Kayo managed to gallop most of the way down the narrow half-mile lane that was fenced on both sides so cattle would not stray. By the time we reached the gate to the pasture, the snow was so deep that Kayo had to slow to a trot. The wind screamed and pelted me from all directions with icy bits of snow. Visibility was down to a few feet. I wasn't afraid because I had been told that horses always know their way home.

Luckily for me, the cattle were huddled together only a few hundred feet from the lane. Almost blinded by the blizzard, I drove them to reach the gate. I tried to count them but each time came up one cow short. I decided to go back to see if I had left one in the pasture.

Either Kayo was in a hurry or he knew what I was looking for. Without my prompting, he trotted past the spot where we had first found the cows. Suddenly I saw the dim form of a cow standing near the fence. Kayo walked up to her and stopped. The cow lowered her head threateningly. Kayo refused to go closer, so I dismounted and began to shuffle around in the snow. The cow threatened us again. Then I stumbled onto her newborn calf lying completely hidden in the snow.

What could I do? The snow was too deep for the calf to walk in it. She was too heavy for me to carry back to the barn. If I left and went for help, we wouldn't be able to find our way back to this spot due to the poor visibility caused by the storm. To make matters worse, the first-time mother seemed to have lost interest in her calf and had joined the other cows now in the lane walking home. Perhaps she understood that Kayo and I were going to help and there was nothing more she could do for her newborn.

I got the idea to put the calf onto Kayo and let him carry her. But would he try to run away with the calf?

To free both hands, I tied the reins together over Kayo's neck. I carried the calf toward him and said, "Whoa," as calmly and firmly as I could. Kayo shied at first but then obediently stood still as I struggled to drape the limp calf over his back.

Kayo continued to stand in place until I gave him the command to "giddy up." He was in control because I didn't have the reins. I could tell that he was trying to go as carefully and smoothly as he could, but it was no use. The snow was now two or more feet deep in places, and I couldn't keep up with him. The calf slid off to the ground. Cushioned by the snow, she wasn't hurt by the fall.

My tears froze to my face as I pleaded with the calf to try and stay on the horse. I begged Kayo to walk even more slowly. Once more I successfully lifted the calf to the back of the waiting pony. Then he did a strange thing. Kayo turned around to head away from the lane. Very carefully and deliberately he pushed me over to the fence and led me to a post.

Aha! I got the message. Kayo wanted me to mount him while the calf was on his back.

I decided to try. Contrary to usual, Kayo braced himself and stood perfectly still while I strained to mount him. After I was astride the pony, I put my knees partly under the dangling calf and also balanced her with my hands.

Kayo waited for me to tell him to move. Then he turned back into the storm toward home. Sometimes the calf would begin to slip, and Kayo would stop until I could balance her again. By the time we neared the barnyard gate, it was almost dark. I could see the forms of my dad and brothers coming to search for me. With worried tones, they asked where I had been.

"Well, I got this calf," I said.

Dad took the calf into the shed and carefully cleaned the snow off her. "She's a good strong heifer," he said. Then he told my brothers to find the mother and for me to take Kayo to his stall and feed him.

I filled Kayo's manger with hay and gave him a double portion of oats. Then I stood by him with my arms around his neck, trying to hug him. He stopped eating for a while as I joyfully sobbed. "We did it, Kayo! We did it!" I hoped my angel understood.

The next day the blizzard was over and the sun shone again. The cattle had trampled paths in the snow. It was Saturday, so I thought this would be a good time to try riding Kayo. Now that we had saved a calf together, I was sure that we were the best of friends. So I jumped on Kayo's back. He took off on a run with me struggling to stay on top of him.

My angel horse had been an angel — only for a day.

Meditation

When has a horse been extra helpful or uncharacteristically easygoing? What does this say to you about the free will of animals?

Horses Can Be Heroes

Laura Cooper
Burwell, Nebraska

*F*or me, there is no greater joy than living and working with horses. The horse bug bit me early in life, and I never recovered. If I can't ride several times a week, or at least hug a horse, the grumpies set in. In my early thirties I even took a job cleaning stalls at a training barn just to have a chance at working my way up. My strategy worked. I spent many years assisting the trainers and sharing my knowledge with students.

Except for a few spills and stepped-on feet, I'd never been seriously hurt. But in 2004 Lady Luck struck out and Murphy's Law walked up to the plate. A young, frisky mare, Glory, caught me off guard, spun, kicked out, and completely snapped my left forearm. Orthopedic surgery repaired the bones, but my agility, timing, and confidence were slow to return.

That autumn, Indian summer lingered with beautiful warm blue skies. I longed to be out on the trails on my gelding, Wind Walker, riding through tall prairie grass and listening to the wind rustle through the drying corn stalks. Instead, from my lawn chair I watched the snow geese and sandhill cranes fly south.

Prior to my broken arm, the tragic death of Wind Walker's stallion father had been my only other crushing blow. Black Watch

Jubilee had been my horse-of-a-lifetime soul mate, so in tune with me that when I sat astride him we had one mind. Jubilee exulted in under-saddle work. He loved sorting and moving cattle, demanding their obedience even when they were twice his weight. But he was extremely gentle with calves, especially with the sick cows. Patience tempered his great heart, and our partnership was a joyful thing to us both. His loss was impossible for me. I had resisted allowing any other horse to fill the void.

When Wind Walker matured, I began natural horsemanship training with him. He surprised me with his willingness to please. The quick-minded little bay gelding made a game out of learning, and he charmed me out of horse cookies and laughter. A strong thread of fear, though, lay beneath his surface eagerness. He wanted to learn and do, but he wouldn't wait for my cues and was terrified of cattle. Nevertheless, we became buds, and he went to work on my lonely heart.

With his charming personality, Wind Walker eventually healed much of the old pain from the loss of Jubilee, and he challenged me to partner up with him. In the past his sire had covered for me when I tired or was lazy with my horsemanship, but this little gelding was his mother's son and demanded that I be a full participant at all times. His reactions to my body language made me improve my skills. We were on the way to becoming a good team when Glory broke my arm.

I'm not the type of person who could tolerate being grounded while I waited for my arm to heal. Wind Walker must have missed our time together as much as I did. I wanted to ride so badly that I tried to groom and saddle him despite my cast. He really got my attention when he started helping me solve the problem of doing the chores one-handed. He lowered his head, closed his eyes, and calmly draped a hoof across my thigh while I cleaned his feet. He stepped under the western saddle as I clumsily shouldered it up onto his back. When I climbed the mounting block, he sidestepped until the stirrup hung exactly where I needed it and then tipped his face to watch me mount. As I healed, he gave his all, offering safety and restoring to me the joy of our being together.

Determined to brush aside my arm injury, I learned how to grab the pitchfork and clean stalls with one good arm, and I continued to try to ride. A stubborn, self-sufficient streak was my downfall. When I injured my knee and foot, it meant that I couldn't get around at all. For the first time in my life, I struggled with helplessness and all that goes with it. And then wisps of fear began to drift in so quietly that I hardly noticed. My body had betrayed me. What if I never fully healed? What if I wasn't up to this anymore? Where had my courage gone?

Laura and Wind Walker

By late November I was finally able to take over light chores, just as my husband's new job started requiring him to be gone during the week. The days were dry and warm. The horses spent most of their time far out in the pasture and came up to the barn only at night for grain. The mercury rose to seventy-two degrees. The horses swished their tails at flies, and sweat gathered under their growing winter coats. November's weather, out here on the Nebraska prairies, always bears watching. After a day of record-breaking heat, the evening forecast called for snow the next morning.

The rising sun made a weak appearance the following morning. After I finished the early chores and hobbled out to the mailbox, snowflakes started sifting down. At two o'clock the wind picked up and the snow fell in earnest. The farm and tree line, a mile to the east, disappeared behind a curtain of blowing white, and tall pine and cedar trees sagged beneath the snow's weight. Standing inside next to our big picture window, I watched drifts pile up in waves around the farm. Bundled against the cold and wind, with my Australian shepherd at my side, I trudged through the drifts toward the barnyard.

I shouldered the barn door open and flipped the light switch. Weak fluorescents quivered in the barn's cold air. Tucking a coffee can of grain between my forearm cast and body, I left the barn, stepped into the deepening drifts, and opened the big gate to the south pasture.

Our small herd of Morgan horses, nearly hidden behind wind-blown snow, somehow heard me when I cupped my mittened hand to my face and called them. Heads came up, hungry whinnies pierced the air, and clouds of snow billowed all around the horses as they bucked and galloped up the hill.

I had more gates to open, so I headed toward the runs. The horses had an established pecking order. Once inside the main gate, they knew which runs were their own. I bent my head to the wind and pushed through the biggest drift to open a gate for the alpha horses, Wind Dancer and Wind Walker. I looked at the horses rushing across the pasture. Much to my surprise, Glory was in the lead.

Glory had been a problem for me ever since she broke my arm. She still brandished her teenage insolence. With a fence between us, it was easy for me to roll my eyes and crack jokes about her "attitudinal." When we were in close proximity to each other, with no fence to separate us, nothing about her attitude or my trepidation was humorous.

Where had my boldness gone? I used to own my own space and easily handle this kind of stuff.

Glory kept her lead as she whipped through the main gate and headed straight for me. I waved her off with my mittened hand as she came at me with lowered head and ears flattened, reaching for the grain can. "Move on, girl. Off with you!" I shouted.

She crowded me up against the fence, turned her rump to me, tucked her tail, and threatened. I waved at her again and growled, "Go on. Get off me!"

Deeper snow was at my backside, and I had nowhere to go. Instinctively I turned and ducked.

A flash of brown fur rushed across the corral. With ears back and teeth flashing, Wind Walker slammed his chest into Glory's haunches and dipped his head to bite her hocks. Then he spun and kicked at her until she ran off. Wind Walker stopped and looked at me with his large, kind dark chocolate eyes. He lifted his muzzle to my face, and his hot breath steamed across my cheek. I leaned against his shoulder and flung my arm over his neck, burying my face in his thick sable coat. His warmth and sweet horse-and-hay scent comforted me as tears filled my eyes.

I was amazed and so grateful for what he had done. This horse, when younger, had been fearful around cattle. Now he had become my little bay hero, showing the heart of his courageous, fearless father by chasing off the belligerent Glory. Wind Walker had come to my rescue when I was in danger and needed him.

Our journey toward unity hasn't been effortless, but we belong to each other now, and it shows. Wind Walker has continued to demand excellence from me as a rider and trainer. He is my four-legged hero. His sire made me believe in my dreams. The son is making me a truly honest, competent horsewoman. He has taught me to hope and persevere. I have been blessed with two great equine teachers.

Meditation

Are horses your heroes? When has a horse come to your rescue in some unexpected way?

Horses and Hurricane Wilma

Sheila Anderson
Wellington, Colorado

*Y*ou would think after two hurricanes in 2004 that my family and I, since we lived in Florida, would have been prepared for Hurricane Wilma in 2005, but we weren't. This storm acted in all ways opposite from a normal hurricane, if there is such a thing. After Hurricane Wilma, once again we had no power, no phone, no gas, no water (we were on a well with an electric pump), and no paycheck.

When the hurricane hit, my horses were in the same barn that had protected them during the previous hurricane season. Sundance is my nine-year-old Appaloosa. I have had him since he was a colt. Chevy, now thirteen, is retired from reining due to having had West Nile virus. Lady Gwennie, our rescued miniature paint mare, rounded out the small herd.

Before the hurricane struck, my human family and the rest of our animal family were safe in our home. At my daughter's insistence we had placed Lady Gwennie in our master bedroom. I thought all was well and that I had done everything I could to prepare for what was to come.

As trees began snapping and the windows in the house bowed from the pressure, it was easy to see that this storm was different. Its power was tremendous. Our house is built on concrete blocks, but it groaned as the wind pushed up against it. Tree branches hit the roof, sounding like boulders.

I don't have hurricane shutters, so I watched from the back window of our house as the entire barn moved off its foundation. Then the barn roof broke off and flew up into the air in one piece. The wind flipped the roof and dropped it over the fence several feet into the backyard. It sounded like a freight train going through a building. Of course, I had opened the stall doors to offer the horses a choice. They bolted as soon as their barn roof gave way.

What made us so lucky is that this happened during the so-called weak side of the storm. The barn roof flipped up and away from the horses. In the stronger backside of the storm, the wind would have been going the other way and the roof would have landed right on them.

The horses galloped to an open area, so for the moment they were safe. I hurried my family to the garage, where we cleared half of it to make a safe space for the horses. When the wind died down a bit, I got a couple ropes, ran to the paddock, and called my horses. They were both trembling.

Frightened horses resort to two instinctive options — fight or flight. When horses are in a fearful state, it is very difficult to handle them and nearly impossible to catch them. Now debris was hitting Sundance and Chevy, and the rain stung like a whip. The wind noise was deafening. I prayed that they would understand I was coming to help them. Their trust in me was about to be put to the ultimate test.

Sundance was afraid to move. When he heard my call, he threw his ears forward and his head up, trying to see where I was. He had to dodge flying debris but heeded my call and came to me. He continued toward me, even when a large pine branch crashed beside him. As soon as he was close enough, he buried his face in my chest and I threw the rope around his neck. The pain of the rain alone was enough to make me cry, let alone the debris hitting us. Weeks later I still had cuts from it. Sundance followed me like a gentleman with Chevy running and snorting behind him. Their trust so far was amazing.

My boyfriend, Charlie, and I were soaking wet by the time we got the horses to the front door of our house. I would have to bring them through the house to get them into our garage since vehicles parked just inside the garage prevented our entering through the outside door. I knew that somehow I would have to walk horses with metal shoes over the tile floor of our home, around a sharp turn, then through the French doors with their large curtains blowing all over because the windows had been broken, past the living room, through the kitchen, and finally into the garage. It would be like walking buffalo across ice.

First I led Sundance. He was terrified, shaking and confused, but he walked quietly beside me. I stepped carefully through the French doors, and he copied my every move. He stayed shoulder to shoulder with me, never once putting tension on the lead rope. One of the curtains whipped across his face, but he didn't flinch. He remained steady through each room. I spoke softly to him. He seemed to understand my every word, doing exactly as I instructed. Finally I placed Sundance in the garage and then went for Chevy.

By now Chevy was hysterical. One of the large pines near him had snapped in the center, making an upside-down canopy. Still attached to its main trunk, the tree section swept across our path like an enormous green broom. The wood cracked and groaned as it moved about. Chevy began to run from me when I came out to get him, or maybe he was heading back to the paddock where he would feel safer.

Right before he got to the paddock gate, I stopped and said, barely loud enough for him to hear, "Come on, Chevy. I will keep you safe. Please trust me, bud."

He stopped immediately, then turned to look at me. For a moment we were almost in a trance. The storm raged around us. He would need to hold back all his instincts and fears. Every muscle of his body was telling him to run to that paddock.

Chevy had little reason to believe in humans and even less reason to trust them. He had been trained hard and shown in reining for nearly his whole life. Scars on his ears and the sides of his belly

Sheila's Chevy and Sundance

are remnants from rough training methods. Even the inside of his mouth is scarred from harsh bits. When he came to us, all of his legs had lumps and bumps from years of constant training. He had to deal with the pain every day. In the first few months of our relationship, he wouldn't let me touch most of his face and neck. He had to be hobbled in a trailer or stall because he kicked so violently.

After Chevy and I got together, I had to spend every moment teaching him to trust me. Then I almost lost him when he nearly died after getting West Nile virus. We had a major breakthrough during that time. All the walls between us melted away, along with his fearful behaviors. During that time Chevy and I had forged a special bond, and I was counting on this relationship now, hoping it would hold up through a hurricane.

Now I walked up to him and slid the rope around his neck. He shook so badly that he could hardly walk straight. He had chosen to stay instead of running away; he was trusting that I would help him. I thanked Chevy for believing in me and started to cry as we made our way back to the house.

By now my daughter had placed some throw rugs down on the floor to help keep Chevy from slipping. He snorted the whole way, but he went with me. He wasn't as calm as Sundance had been nearing the blowing curtains, so I gently placed my hand on his neck and softly spoke to him. He looked at me, his eyes as big as saucers, and continued to follow. He kept his eyes on me until we were through the French doors. He walked very carefully, following the path that I made ahead of him. As we entered the kitchen the pots, just over head, were banging in the wind. He hesitated for a moment but with my gentle encouragement walked under them. He stayed very close, shaking and snorting until we reached the last door in the house. When I opened the door to the garage, the two horses greeted each other with deafening whinnies.

It took about ten minutes for them to settle down. They only had enough room to stand next to each other. Not once did they try to kick or bite each other, which they normally would have done. Instead they spent their time nosing into my boxes, taking my laundry out of the dryer, and dumping over almost anything they could. They had great fun keeping warm and dry in the garage while Lady Gwennie continued to rearrange our master bedroom.

Thank goodness I took them out of the barn. The backside of the storm finished off the rest of it. All we could do was to shut off the doors to half the house, fearing the windows wouldn't hold, and wait in our safe room. We heard crashing and banging; we could feel the wind inside those rooms. Water came in sideways through the bottoms of the closed windows.

After many hours we were able to venture outside to see the destruction. The entire neighborhood had changed. The amount of branches we eventually removed from my two acres could have filled several tractor trailers.

If you know horses, you know how much they run on instinct. It was a big feat for them to come with me through a heavily landscaped backyard while being beaten by wind, rain, and tree debris. Then they had to walk on slick surfaces into an enclosed area where they were squished together for hours. All that time we had spent together prior to this storm — trailer-loading lessons, ground work, and flat-out friendship — had helped us that day.

One of my biggest lessons I learned from Hurricane Wilma is that what you do on a daily basis is what counts the most. If you build love and trust or destroy it, a little at a time, day by day, when danger or tragedy strikes, you will experience the effects of your daily actions. Now I spend every day building love and trust with everything and everyone. I learned from Sundance and Chevy that you never know when you will need to rely on those essential foundations of a relationship.

Meditation

Who could you build love and trust with today? Would it make a difference when life blows the winds of change?

The Little Sorrel Mare Who Saved My Life

Dawn Nelson
Creston, Washington

The little sorrel mare was the ugliest horse I had ever seen. I was eight years old when she came to our ranch, a starved and horribly neglected two-year-old. She was so skinny that her backbone stuck up a good inch or so, and her head looked four times the size of her body. The bone structure on this little mare was light, to say the least. When she walked, she practically dragged her head on the ground. Pride was just one of the things that she lacked.

I asked my grandfather why he brought her home. He explained that all of the mare's ugliness was just top-dressing. With a little food and love, she would become a great-looking little horse. Since my mare, B, was twenty-five and arthritic, he thought I would soon need a new horse.

So, the truth was out. Grandpa expected that runty little stitch of a horse to be the replacement for my fourteen-hundred-pound mare, B, who was a top-notch foundation-bred roping horse. I wanted nothing to do with that ugly little wannabe replacement.

For two years I ignored the little mare. I refused to catch her for anyone to ride. I didn't want anyone to even see her on our place. I would give B a can of grain and stay to make sure she ate all of it. But I never paid any attention to whether the little sorrel mare got all her food, or if the other ranch horses chased her away before she could finish eating.

I worked odd jobs at the local veterinarian's office, mowed lawns, and rode racehorses at the track for twenty-five cents a day to buy minerals and vitamins for B. But I never gave any to the little sorrel mare. Heck, I didn't even name her at that time. She was just known as "that little sorrel mare." She turned out to be quite a little riding horse, but she was too small for the adults, so mostly my brother rode her.

Looking back now, I am ashamed of treating any living thing with so little compassion. I was a cruel and hateful preteen, to say the least. Ten years old and not a lick of good sense. Nobody seemed to notice that I never wanted anything to do with the sorrel or that I would have preferred her never to have come to our ranch. I left her feeding to my grandfather. I never hit or starved her. I just refused her what I could have easily given — nutrients and love.

It all changed one night while I sat out in the pasture, holding B's head in my arms while her eyes closed for the last time. I cried long into the night, refusing to leave B's side, until my father buried her the following morning. The veterinarian told my father that B's death was due to old age. Her heart had just given up. The vet's words were hard for me to believe. One thing that B never did was give up.

B could keep up with any horse, gaited or not. She loved me like her own child. And I loved her more than any child loves her mother. She was my babysitter while my parents worked. She protected me when my brother and his friends picked on me. At the time of her death I was ten years old and devastated over losing the best friend I had ever known.

As I watched Dad take B's body away the next morning, I collapsed in the horse corral, crying for the rides I would never have with her again. I had to accept the fact that I could no longer tell all my problems to B or look into her soft, brown eyes and know everything would be all right. I swore I would *never* own a horse again or ride one for as long as I lived!

Suddenly a soft, caring little wet nose nudged me. Because I was so upset, I didn't think about how much I disliked that little sorrel mare. When she tried to comfort me, I turned and buried my face in her neck and sobbed. She just stood there, and in her own way gave me a hug. We stayed in the horse corral together for most of the day. She never walked away from me once. She listened to all my problems and even contributed a few of hers. Looking into her eyes, I realized how much she loved me and needed my love. To this day, I still would swear that I saw a tear in her eye for B.

Forgetting my vow to never ride or own another horse as long as I lived, and because of the kindness the sorrel mare had shown, I decided to start riding her. She had grown into quite a good-looking young horse. Her body was starting to fill out. I rode her bareback with a halter and lead rope most of the time, sometimes with nothing at all. We both knew what the other was thinking, and I had no fear of her ever hurting or running off with me.

Soon we were inseparable and went everywhere together. I would skip school and take her up to the meadow to eat. I bought every vitamin and mineral made for helping horses to grow and everything else I could afford to make her life better. I still couldn't think of a good-enough name for her so I continued to call her "that little sorrel mare." However, the "little" part of her nickname was vanishing rapidly.

I spent the whole summer running wild with the sorrel mare, and I started calling her Sorrel for short. Looking back, that was the

Dawn's Gadget

best summer of my life. I still missed B terribly, but I knew she had taught Sorrel all she could. I began showing Sorrel in 4-H and at a junior rodeo. Grandpa told me I needed a real name for her so she could hold her head up high when we entered the arena and they said our names, but nothing seemed to fit her. Nothing seemed good enough.

That summer Sorrel beat everybody at barrels and poles. She was wonderful with her quick turns and fast takeoffs. Sorrel seemed to have a slight smile on her face every time we won an event. Calf roping was a cinch with a quick little horse like Sorrel under me. However, I could never tie goats. The first time she saw a goat, Sorrel came to a sudden stop, stared at it for the longest time, and wouldn't budge.

Sorrel marched in parades. She was getting quite big. Her sleek body glistened as we pranced down the highway in front of everybody. She would arch her neck and walk as if she were carrying the queen of England. During two summers, we traveled with no hassles or problems all over the ten-mile circumference around our little canyon, going up into the mountains for days on end and coming down for ice cream bars and apples.

The fall that I was twelve and Sorrel was six, we were chasing cows up in the high pasture. We ran through some thick brush, trying to get around a cow, when suddenly Sorrel came to an abrupt stop. I thought maybe she was getting a little tired, so I promised her as soon as we turned the cow we could rest but we had to keep moving right now. The cows were getting away. I knew that if I lost track of them in the brush and timber, it would be hard to find them again. I'd have to follow their tracks through the brush, get off my horse, and study the ground very carefully to see which way they went.

So I kicked Sorrel and tried to get her moving. Every time I kicked, she nipped my leg. I started to get off to lead her. Before I could move far, she again turned and nipped my leg. She was acting so strange — all stretched out and refusing to move a foot. And she was pulling brush out by the roots. She must have pulled six bushes out before I could see what she saw. We were straddling a fifteen-foot-deep mine hole that was about six feet across. My grandfather had told me that the land had been mined long before I was ever thought of, and holes had been dug everywhere. He always warned me to watch out for the holes. Twelve of them were already staked out, so I knew where they were. This one had never been staked. The brush was so thick that no one saw it. The leftover mine hole was in a place where we seldom went, and no roads led to it.

I had no clue if we were going to be able to jump over the hole. Sorrel had propped her front feet up on a log that had fallen over it. Her back feet were barely on its edge. Visions of my parents finding us lying dead at the bottom of this old mine hole flashed through my head.

Suddenly Sorrel stood straight up on her hind feet. Before I knew what was happening, she had spun around until we were clear of the hole.

That afternoon I walked her the whole way home. She deserved a huge break. I knew she was tired, and she needed a long walk with a nice, loosened cinch. Besides, I was shaking so much that I'm not sure I could have stayed on if I had ridden her home. I had found a kindred spirit in Sorrel and that one great horse that a person can find only once in her life.

At last I came up with a name for the little sorrel. I called her Gadget, after Inspector Gadget, the cartoon hero, who could invent gadgets to save himself and others. Gadget fit her because of all the nifty ways she knew for getting us out of tight fixes. In addition to saving us from falling in the mine hole, many times Gadget got me out of trouble with my mom. Mom couldn't refuse Gadget anything, so if Mom was mad at me, I would just say, "Gadget made me do it." Mom would laugh and say, "Well, if Gadget did it, than I guess it's all right."

I promised Gadget I would always take care of her, as she had taken care of me. I told her that I would make sure no one ever separated us.

About a year after finding the mine hole, Gadget and I were riding home from my girlfriend's house at one in the morning. Without warning, Gadget darted to the left, out from under a tree, and took off running. I tried to slow her down. I was bareback and carrying my backpack with a baby bunny that I had found injured along the trail. Gadget took hold of the bit and kept running. I held on for dear life.

I heard something thumping the ground behind us. In the moonlight I could see a form chasing us. I couldn't quite make out what it was until we crossed the open meadow. Then I saw a cougar. My heart kept beat with the pounding of his feet behind us. My imagination saw him way better than my eyes did — long and sleek with white teeth longing for the taste of horse, baby bunny, and girl flesh.

It was another mile until we would reach the flat fields by our house. I didn't know if Gadget could keep up this pace long enough. She ran fast down that mountain, maneuvering over rocks, trees, and only God knows what else. The cougar finally stopped chasing us, and we made it safely home — Gadget, baby bunny, and me.

Four years ago, while I was riding Gadget through the rough country during fall roundup, I was chasing a group of cows down a shale slide. Gadget stopped and tried to go backward, but she was having no luck. We were sliding down the side of a slick mountain, and stopping was the last thing we could do.

A string of barbed wire was strung across the bottom of the mountain, beneath the rocks. Gadget slid into the wire. It caught on her hind feet. She tried with all her might to stay in one place. I got off of her but slid halfway down the mountain on the shale rock. I was able to inch my way back up the mountain and break her loose from the barbed wire. I had no fence pliers with me, so I had to twist the barbed wire back and forth between my hands until it snapped. Together, we slid the rest of the way down the mountain. All I could do was to try and stay ahead of her.

I checked her out at the bottom, figuring she would be cut to pieces, but she had no blood or cuts whatsoever. Most horses would have freaked out in that situation and been badly cut. I hate to think what would have happened to me if Gadget had panicked. But when I am sitting atop one of the best little cow horses I have ever met, I know that I am safe from whatever might come our way.

Gadget taught me compassion and love, that beauty doesn't have to be seen by others, and that it really is only skin-deep. Most of all, she made my grandfather's words sink in: With a good horse under you, there is nothing you can't accomplish. Because of her, when I became a teenager I never drank or did drugs. I knew she would know. I've heard that horses can feel a person's moods and they know how you feel. I never wanted to hurt her because of some stupid five-second high.

In the days since her retirement from hard riding, Gadget has taught many children to ride with confidence. When she competes at the fair with a child, everybody knows her name and that most likely the child who is riding her will win. I have been offered a lot of money for Gadget — $25,000 was the highest yet — but I would never sell her. She will live out her days on our cattle ranch. She has earned the reward of being cared for in her old age. Gadget has touched the lives of hundreds in our community. She has the biggest heart of any horse I have ever known.

I often wonder what would have happened had Grandpa not seen the good in that scrawny little sorrel mare. I tell my husband that when they bury me to put an apple in the coffin with me so that I can give it to Gadget when I see her again. I know that I will see her again. For all good horses, there is a heaven.

In loving memory of the great man who brought Gadget home to me, Grandpa Pete Singer (1914–2006). On the day Grandpa died, I heard the great news from our vet that Gadget is to have twins.

Meditation

Who have you misjudged or prejudged? Could you reevaluate the relationship and discover what it might truly have to offer?

Mule Intelligence

Fred Wickert
Gilboa, New York

*A*s a boy, I lived on a small farm near Syracuse, New York, around the time World War II began. My father and I farmed the hard way in those days, mostly doing everything by hand with the help of a team of mules named Julius and Caesar. What a great thrill it was for me, as an eight-year-old, to be driving a team of mules. None of my sisters could do that, and it made me feel very grown up. Julius and Caesar were my friends. Every chance I got, I petted their noses and fed them little goodies, such as a lump of sugar, a slice of bread, or a handful of green clover.

One day Dad and I were building an electric fence for a temporary pasture on a gentle slope in the rear portion of the farm. It was a hot day. We hitched the mule team to a box-type wagon where we carried wire, fence posts, and tools. As we worked, Julius began pawing at the ground. Dad was afraid that if the mule kept doing this, some of his harness would get damaged and have to be mended.

After each episode of Julius digging in the ground, Dad would get him to stop and then return to fence building. After a few moments Julius would paw at the ground again. Dad would speak to him by scratching Julius's head between the ears and asking him to settle down and stand quietly. Julius would stop pawing until Dad resumed work. Then the mule would start scraping at the ground with his hooves again.

Dad was puzzled by Julius's behavior. He could see nothing wrong that would cause the mule to do this. But soon the reason for Julius's mule stubbornness became clear.

With his continual pawing, Julius had dug a hole almost a foot deep. Water from a small spring, which we had not known existed, began flowing into the hole. The water was cool and clean, being filtered by a small deposit of gravel that we also did not know was there. Julius and Caesar took turns drinking their fill of the water. We never understood how Julius knew water was in that spot. But he did.

Our farm adjoined property that was owned by a country club named Drumlins. It provided fine dining, a ballroom, a golf course, and in the winter months an ice-skating rink, ski slope, and a ski jump overlooking the golf course. In the summer months hay grew on the ski slope. The Drumlins's golf course crew had a tractor with a mowing machine. The crew mowed the hay on the ski slope in late summer so it would not later interfere with skiing by protruding through the snow. My father made arrangements with Drumlins's management to take the mowed hay from the hill.

In those days the process of haying was to use a dump-rake machine drawn by the mules. We raked the cut hay into windrows, which were then rolled up by hand with a pitchfork into a pile called a haycock. I would drive the team of mules with our hay wagon between rows of haycocks. My father would throw those haycocks onto the wagon with a pitchfork until the load became so high that no more could be piled on.

One day we were at the top of the ski slope with a full load of hay. On one end of the ski slope, a double track on a steep hill descended to the golf course below. It was too steep to go down with a full load of hay. Our practice was to stop at the top of the hill and chain the wheels on the wagon. We would wrap the chain through the wheel spokes and around the axle. In that way the wheels would not turn. Instead they would slide along the ground with a length of chain in front of them, acting as a brake for the heavy load that was sliding down the hill behind the mule team.

On this particular trip we had not yet chained the wheels when the team of mules suddenly stopped. Julius, the mule on the left side of the team, sat down. Dad investigated to determine why he had done this. He discovered that the whippletree, a crossbeam to which the team is hitched for pulling the wagon, had broken at the point where the long pin went through to hold it fast to the tongue of the wagon. Had the team continued forward, the pole would have come free from the neck yoke bar, and the wagon would have freewheeled down the mountain, ending in disaster. The mules and I could all have been killed.

My father and I swiftly chained and blocked the wagon wheels while the mules patiently kept it from rolling down the hill. They had just saved my life and theirs.

After we secured the wagon so that it could not roll down the hill, we unhitched the mules and drove them to some shade under a pair of apple trees amid tall sweet clover. There they enjoyed a well-deserved rest while we made a trip to the barn for another whipple-tree.

We would never know how Julius knew the whippletree had broken and how he and Caesar understood what to do to stop the wagon and hold it. Between the two of them, Julius had always been the leader, and Caesar would follow. In this instance, Julius had sat down while Caesar remained standing. Caesar, who was bigger and taller, had leaned his weight backward to the rear to help hold the weight of the wagon. The level of their teamwork was impressive.

I am truly grateful for the actions of Julius and Caesar that day. I wince every time I hear or see the words *dumb animals*, because these two mules taught me that animals often possess wisdom and intelligence beyond our own. Had they not, this story could never have been written. They are my unsung heroes.

Meditation

When have you seen a mulish stubbornness turn into quiet determination and a show of courage? What faults might you be seeing in a person or an animal that are actually their best qualities in a crisis?

Fashion

Susan Chernak McElroy
Teton Valley, Idaho

he dark bay thoroughbred mare who backed uncertainly from the rear of the too-small horse trailer was the tallest horse I'd ever seen. Her shoulders were like crested mountains and seemed to touch the clouds. Against the clear blue Wyoming sky, she was the color of deep wet soil. My hand brushed her neck as all four of her feet made contact with the earth again, and she shuddered beneath my touch and shifted sideways to get away from me.

Fashion was my first and only horse, given to me by my Native American friend and teacher, David Bearclaw. In Native tradition, the gift of a horse is not to be taken lightly. It is a gift of great power, great honor. And so I was in no position to refuse the gift, although it came in a package I would have never, ever chosen myself. You see, my fantasy horse was always short, tough, and willing — a mustang maybe, or a hardy mountain pony with legs like concrete pillars and a back as broad as a sofa. Fashion was certainly not short, tough, or on that particular July day, willing. She was a tall, old thoroughbred mare long off the racetrack, where she had once had a rare chance at greatness.

Standing beside her in the driveway, I could not help but notice that her right knee was thick with gnarled bone and arthritis, the result of a fracture that had taken her off the track and put her into early retirement more than fifteen years before. David had told me about it. She would be a good "first horse" for me, he had said. That knee would keep her from living her destiny as the swift, regal descendant of the legendary Man O' War and prevent her from carrying me on wild rides of which I was incapable.

From the lumpy burl on her knee, my eyes went next to her feet. They were long and cracked, and she danced nervously in my driveway on clumpy, hurt toes like a ballerina in wooden clogs. I could feel apprehension begin to rise up lavalike from my ankles. Nervous diarrhea had splattered the backs of her legs. She was thin. Her mane and tail were a dusty mass of tangles, and her coat was dull. Corralled for two years at the home of a man too frequently out of town, she was a poster child for neglect — not abuse, mind you, just neglect, like the neglect most of us have been guilty of at one time or another, to one being or another. She had been David's horse for many years, coming with him from the horse farms in Kentucky, where he had been a top trainer. A few years earlier he had given her to a friend, as a riding horse for his wife. But the wife never rode her, and the man's work took him away from home more and more.

Neglect settles down in a particularly harsh way on an eighteen-year-old horse. Gone is the instant bounce-back of supple bones, athletic flesh, firm skin. I felt it myself in my late, late forties — that shocking and ominous loss of instant regeneration after a long day in the garden or a night or three of fitful sleep.

I stepped toward my gift horse and offered her my hand. "Hello, Fashion. Welcome home." She turned her face away and thrust her high head even higher into the air. Her breath came in impatient snorts, and she scampered on the end of her lead rope. I could have been a gnat, for all her interest in me. David placed the lead rope into my hands. "Take the lead. She's yours now." Trepidation mounting, I took hold of this 16.2 hands of old, bony mare who had often stood covered with flowers in the winner's circle. "She could have been one of the great ones," David had told me, "if not for that knee." He looked at me and smiled broadly, nodding his head at the two of us as though he knew something that I didn't. With mixed emotions of gratitude and dread, I walked my gift horse up to the barn.

That night in bed, unable to sleep, I asked myself why this mare had come to me. What an utterly unlikely pair we made: me, a complete greenhorn, and she, a hot-blooded track horse with a bad knee and a distant attitude. What had David been thinking to give this horse to me? She'd kill me, I thought. If I didn't expire falling off her back, which was as high as a house, the vet bills to get her back on her feet would preclude me ever buying groceries again, and I'd starve to death.

I had yet another fear that I could not articulate at that time, a bigger fear that lurked far below my level of consciousness. I was afraid of her age. To me, her eighteen years signified the end of life, infirmity, crumbling, as much as my coming fiftieth year signified the same in my own life. My mother, past eighty, has a proverb she has been fond of since her midseventies, and it had sunk into me far deeper than the level of my hearing: "Getting old is hell. Don't get old."

My horsewoman friend Kathy says that most horses in our country do not live to be eighteen. Mostly it is because we do not let them. Old horses and old people are marginal and worthless in our culture, their "usefulness" to us as dead as their youth. After a long night of fitful dreaming, I knew only two things for certain about Fashion and myself. First, I could not give her back. She was my gift horse, and that was that. Second, I trusted that she had been important to Dave, and I trusted Dave. His parting words to me were, "She is the best. That's all. You'll see." There was nothing to be done, then, but to care for her and to see where time would take us.

The sun was shining when I walked up to the barn that morning. Fashion stood like a dark tree rooted in the middle of the pasture, never looking my way until I stood in front of her with a halter and lead rope. And even then, all she offered was a passing glance that took me in and dismissed me all in the same instant. She was easy to halter and to lead, and I tied her up to a fence post and began working the knots out of her mane and the dirt out of her coat while she gazed with a blank expression at the mountains behind the house. Yet when I put a soft dust brush to her forehead, she came back into her body instantly, thrusting her head up and down against the length of the bristles over and over to get at every itch that ever was. I held the brush tightly in place, feeling the enormous power of her neck pushing against my hands. When she was done, she blew a blast of damp air from her nose and sighed heavily. Her eyes went back to the hills, and I once again felt as unnoticed as a barn fly flitting around her face.

What I wanted most from a horse was a relationship, a connection. The riding would have been a secondary thrill. I longed for Fashion to take notice of me, to like me instantly and completely, as my dogs had always liked me. But my Flicka fantasies faded as quickly as the waning summer days. She was not — how shall I say it? — effusive in her affections. She was not interested in the bonding that I sought. She had come to me after a long history that I could only imagine, and her personhood was set and secure. My own history — equally unknown to her — had carved me into a seeker of recognition. In all areas of my life, I seek to be known, to be seen. It has become my personal antidote for loneliness. And so I brought the needs of my own near half century of living to the table with Fashion and was crestfallen that she was not interested in the intimacy and affirmation that I was trying to dish up between us.

For the rest of the summer, I resigned myself to being a care giver, for that was the relationship she allowed me.

My unlikely conglomeration of treatments, special supplements, exercises, and effort came together in a mysterious alchemical blending, and as the summer harvest ripened, Fashion began to look like the queen she must have once been. I spent hours brushing her and humming away in the shade of the barn, loving the rich, dusty smell of her and the heat of her skin against my hands. She had stopped her habit of moving away from the brushes, and sometimes I would see her faraway eyes slip into a contented doze, the lids like half-moons over the brown planets of her eyes. My favorite horse song was "Goodbye old Paint, I'm leaving Cheyenne," and I sang it incessantly. By fall, I think even the barn wasps knew the words.

Fashion took on a shine, with big golden dapples spread in a lush sheen over her liver-colored coat. Someone loaned me a very old saddle and a hackamore, and, overtaken by a total lack of good sense, I began to take Fashion out for short rides alone in the foothills beyond our house. One afternoon as we descended the hill behind my barn, she began leaping side to side in a burst of fall frolicking, and I jettisoned out of control off her back like a stone out of a slingshot. She stopped, stunned, and put her head down to sniff me. I don't imagine she had ever seen a rider become unglued so fast, and it was a revelation to both of us. In all our future rides, I somehow managed to stay aboard, but not like a rider, really. More like a determined tick.

I began to see why David believed that Fashion and I would be good for each other. Elder horses have a quality that is hard to put a name to, a certain sense of composure and acceptance that serves true greenhorns well. When we rode together, I always felt as though I were going on an outing with Everywoman's mythic grandma — the grandma who exudes comfort and wisdom and whose stance in the world is one of no nonsense and no whining.

With such a grandma, we are emotionally safe forever.

As any good mother (grandmother?) will do, Fashion began the immense task of teaching me how to spend safe time in the company of others — in this case, horse others. She taught me how to mind my manners by modeling for me how flawless she was at minding hers.

David told me she had been born self-assured and royally confident. So strong was her sense of self that my constant fumbling and lack of horse skills had no effect on her whatsoever. Fashion trusted herself in a way that was refreshing and thought provoking for me. In her presence, I wondered often what it must be like to live so comfortably in one's own skin, and I sensed that the ripening of age had some part in the process. While my mother told me that growing old is just pure hell, Fashion told me something different, although at the time, I thought she was teaching me only about horses and riders.

In caring for my gift horse, I reconnected daily to the joy of giving simply for its own sake. Some animals you care for clearly appreciate what you do for them, but this was not the case with Fashion, for whom I was simply "the staff." In her eyes, I was put on Earth to care for horses, and she was generously enabling me to do that. But on one day late in the fall, when the mountain breezes were crisp and the sun was as yellow as lemons, my gift horse graced me with an unexpected, immense gift of her own. This gift made all my fussing and tending and caretaking pale in comparison.

It began simply enough on that sunny fall morning when I spotted Fashion lying in a heap in the west corner of the pasture. It was her favorite spot for sunning. Halter in hand, I headed her way in hopes of an early ride before the sun got too hot. Usually Fashion would hurry to her feet the moment she sensed me coming, but this day she remained down, fairly groaning with the joy of the early sun on her side and face.

Caught up in the quiet bliss of the moment, I moved quietly to her head and knelt down beside her. "Want to go for a ride, pretty one?" She opened one liquid brown eye and gazed into my face. Then her sleepy eye spotted the blue halter. With a heavy sigh she nosed the halter aside and placed her enormous jug of a head on my lap. The eye closed, her rubbery lips twitched, and a soft snore rumbled from her chest. I stroked her peach-soft cheeks and rubbed her leaflike ears between my fingers. The solid weight of her head sank deep against my legs and stomach. I could feel the warmth of her face and the hardness of her jaw. She twitched her ears at the buzz of a fly, and her snoring deepened. The summer grass was old now, bent dry and yellow beneath us.

Time ran down and stopped, and we rested together in a moment that was complete and perfect. Emotions shivered through me as I pressed my palm to Fashion's face again and again, drinking up the rare, precious moment of feminine intimacy, friendship, and recognition. Finally she had seen me, and the sweetness of her gift to me was like cold water after a four-day fast. It struck me so deeply that I would never forget it — this moment of being seen after trying so hard, almost desperately, to make myself visible.

When we at last rose to our feet — stiffly, as old girls do — we had changed. In those few sacred moments, we had become the companions David must have been seeing in his mind's eye when he placed the lead rope of a gift horse into my uncertain and unknowing hands. I know the old saying "Never look a gift horse in the mouth" has to do with long teeth and aging and gratitude. But the saying is not quite right. Instead, it should be simply, "Never doubt a gift horse." Ever.

Meditation

What have horses taught you about endurance and perseverance? Has observing an animal age taught you anything about handling the aging process?

Ask Zeke

Dear Zeke,

How have horses throughout history had the courage to ride bravely into battle? Isn't it a horse's instinct to run away from danger?

Sincerely,
Battle Fatigued

Dear Battle Fatigued,

Even though horses are skittish by nature and show fright by rearing up and galloping away, we are the only creatures on earth who unflinchingly and knowingly face the loss of our own lives in battle. With great pride, we carry brave warriors on our backs and charge toward enemies that would kill them and us. Horses do this out of love.

No matter what humans might think about the cruel ways they have devised to train us, horses are not afraid of being punished if they don't obey. We do as humans command, even unto death, because purpose and destiny rule our actions. Fear is a distant second as reason enough to put our lives on the line or our wills in subservience.

We know who we are and why we are here. Horses have never forgotten the call of dedication and service to the greater good. This is why we endure.

Courageously yours,
Zeke

CHAPTER FOUR

Spiritual Connection
and the Afterlife

For you shall have a covenant
with the stones of the field,
and the beasts of the field
shall be at peace with you.

— Job 5:23

$\mathcal{B}$y 1897 Dr. William Key had trained himself to be a veterinarian and his horse, the Beautiful Jim Key, to be a consummate showman. The man, who used to be a slave, and the horse, who had been sold to P. T. Barnum's circus and abused into learning tricks, formed a loving team when Dr. Key bought Beautiful Jim for forty dollars. With great kindness and patience, Dr. Key trained the horse to be an entertainer and an educator, demonstrating the rewards of kindness to animals. He brought Beautiful Jim into his house, and the young horse lived with Dr. Key as a toilet-trained pet for seven years. Then the two of them went on tour to amaze ten million people in venues all over the country, including the 1904 St. Louis

World's Fair and the White House. In her review of the book about the life of these devoted friends, *Beautiful Jim Key* by Mim Eichler Rivas (William Morrow, 2006), Karin Winegar writes, "Jim Key's ability to read, count, and recognize dozens of Bible quotations — at least those about horses — provoked rabbis, ministers, academicians, and common folk to debate: Do animals have minds? Do they have souls?"[1]

The debate about animals and souls continues today. People develop unique bonds with horses and other animals, and experience them as spiritual beings with whom they can communicate telepathically. Throughout these relationships, the animals prove time and again that they are much more than physical bodies. Their spiritual essence is as divine sparks of God. After the horse's death, the soul, the part that didn't die, often makes itself known to the person by continuing to be present either through a dream, a vision, a symbol, or some other manifestation that the person recognizes as the horse. Often this is when the skeptical mind kicks in, fueled by questions and doubts about the authenticity of spiritual experiences in general and horses as the catalysts in particular. Those who cross the bridge between mind and spirit reap the benefits of the realization that death is a transition from physical to invisible realities.

Throughout history religious, spiritual, and cultural traditions have told stories of animals used by the Divine to bring more love, guidance, and protection into the lives of those humble enough to receive this help. Animals, with their ability to love unconditionally without judgment or pretense, become ideal messengers, open to hearing the whispers of Divine Spirit.

In the Bible the story of Balaam and his donkey provides one of the most dramatic examples of an equine messenger, an "angel animal":

God was angry that Balaam was going, and as Balaam was riding along on his donkey, accompanied by his two servants, an angel of the Lord stood in the road to bar his way. When the donkey saw the angel standing there holding a sword, it left the road and turned into the fields. Balaam beat the donkey and brought it back onto the road. Then the angel stood where the road narrowed between two vineyards and had a stone wall on each side. When the donkey saw the angel, it moved over against the wall and crushed Balaam's foot against it. Again, Balaam beat the donkey. Once more the angel moved ahead; he stood in a narrow place where there was no room at all to pass on either side. This time, when the donkey saw the angel, it lay down. Balaam lost his temper and began to beat the donkey with his stick. Then the Lord gave the donkey the power of speech, and it said to Balaam, "What have I done to you? Why have you beaten me these three times?"

Balaam answered, "Because you have made a fool of me! If I had a sword, I would kill you."

The donkey replied, "Am I not the same donkey on which you have ridden all your life? Have I ever treated you like this before?"

"No," he answered.

Then the Lord let Balaam see the angel standing there with his sword; and Balaam threw himself face downward on the ground. The angel demanded, "Why have you beaten your donkey three times like this? I have come to bar your way, because you should not be making this journey. But your donkey saw me and turned aside three times. If it hadn't, I would have killed you and spared the donkey."

Balaam replied, "I have sinned. I did not know that you were standing in the road to oppose me; but now if you think it is wrong for me to go on, I will return home." (Numbers 22:22–25 Good News Translation)

A Buddhist tale relates the story of a mighty horse who served King Brahmadatta, the ruler of Benares in northern India. The horse had been born in western India and was known to be intelligent, loyal, trustworthy, and wise, an enlightened being whose name was Knowing-one. When seven neighboring kings declared war on King Brahmadatta and surrounded Benares with their cavalries, he called for his champion knight to represent him on the battlefield. The knight's only request was to ride Knowing-one into battle to save the country from its enemies.

Knowing-one was loyal to the king, but he also knew that killing was not the true course to victory. He spoke to the champion knight and told him that he would show him a new way to win wars without killing. The knight agreed to let the horse take the lead.

Knowing-one charged into battle against the first king, who had laid siege to the city. He fought with the speed of lightning and the might of a hundred elephants, easily capturing the king without killing a single soldier. Knowing-one did this with four more kings and their armies. Upon capturing the sixth king, he received a terrible wound as one of the king's bodyguards thrust a sword deep into the horse's side. The champion knight, upon seeing the terrible wound, almost switched horses, but Knowing-one convinced him to continue the battle with him. He knew that the knight would revert to the old ways of slaughtering men and horses. He was determined to capture the seventh king alive and show the knight and the king that peaceful means could be used to defeat their enemies.

After the champion knight rode Knowing-one to victory, capturing the seventh king, all the armies laid down their weapons and asked for peace.

Knowing-one lay dying as a tearful King Brahmadatta visited his stall. The horse's last wishes were that the seven captive kings not be killed, that the king reward the champion knight, and that from this day on the king only do wholesome, generous deeds, killing no other living being.

At Knowing-one's death, King Brahmadatta brought the seven kings before him, where all honored the horse who had defeated them without spilling a drop of their blood. Never again did the kings fight with one another, living in peace from that day forward. This taught everyone that peace can be attained through peaceful means.[2]

If you are open to their deeper meanings, the stories in this chapter will take you on peaceful spiritual adventures. They will inspire you to think about your own connections with horses as spiritual beings and teachers.

What spiritual connections will be revealed as you read the stories that others tell? Will the thin veil that separates the visible from the invisible lift for you too?

A Lovely Freedom

Holly Williams
Greenfield, New Hampshire

*E*ver since I was a small child, I have been drawn to horses. Finally, at the age of twelve, after years of begging my parents and babysitting to earn money, I became the proud owner of the most beautiful palomino mustang mare in the whole world. I grew up reading authors Marguerite Henry and Walter Farley and every horse book I could scare up in the library. Because of my fascination with Marguerite Henry's exciting tales of ponies living on Chincoteague Island, I named the mare Misty, after one of the rough-and-tumble pony characters in the books.

The pure joy and excitement of having my own horse through my junior high and high school years and riding with my best friends — Ann, Sheryl, and Kathy — sustained me during a very difficult time in my life. I had troubles at home, and Misty and my friends provided the companionship and comic relief I needed.

Misty was my spiritual guide and most trusted companion. On her back, I believed I could go anywhere. I could dare to be myself, to dream and be happy in a way I hadn't known was possible. It was a lovely freedom that she and I shared. My beloved golden girl gave me a sense of inner peace and confidence that blossomed and grew each time we were together. We were inseparable in heart, mind, and soul. When we were together, all seemed right in the world.

Twenty-one years and many horses later, I was looking forward to a day of competing with my young thoroughbred gelding, Elucidar, or Foley, as he was known to all his friends. He had been bred, born, and trained here at Muzzey Hill Farm, our horse farm.

We were making our way to Massachusetts to perform our Second Level 4 and Third Level 1 dressage tests. I enjoy showing and always look forward to a day of competition devoted to being with my horse, riding, and solely concentrating on what I most love doing.

Our Third Level test was scheduled for 8:40 in the morning, and the Second Level test was six hours later. Our warm-up for the first ride was uneventful, which was no small miracle. Foley hated being crowded in with other horses. He had bucked until he was about thirteen years old. Once Foley was in the arena, though, he knew his task and settled in. He too enjoyed performing. It was always a pleasure and relief to feel him relax and start listening to me. I could sense his trust and confidence grow as our ride progressed.

Our first test that day went fine. The trot work was energetic and balanced. I had trouble with the simple change of lead and counter canter, but all was okay. We placed fourth.

I occupied the next six hours by taking care of Foley, preparing for the next test, hand-grazing Foley on some tasty grass, and hanging out and talking with friends who passed our way. Then we warmed up and made our way toward the dressage arena, riding quietly around the perimeter, listening for the bell or whistle to signal our entrance.

Looking back at the actual paper test that day, I see that we made a nice straight entrance and went on to show our collected trot, travers right and left, ten-meter circles, shoulder-in, and medium trot. These movements help the horses to become better balanced, flexible, and supple throughout the body and develop strength in the hindquarters for carrying power. The idea is to build a harmonious communication between horse and rider, always a work in progress, with the horse's welfare coming first.

Foley had a smooth, almost slow-motion way of performing, and everything felt good. After the second shoulder-in to the left, we approached the judge's box for a halt and rein-back, anticipating the free walk across the diagonal. As we came through the corner of the short end of the arena, I was looking across the diagonal toward the opposite end of our twenty-by-sixty-meter area.

Holly and Foley

My eyes were drawn to the sky, and it seemed as if the heavens beckoned to me. I felt as though we were walking up an endless stairway to heaven. Perfect calm spread through my body. A heightened sense of clarity and inner peace transformed into a genuine knowledge that all was right and good in the world. Inwardly I moved on the wave of a magnificent ascension, leading toward the beginning of time and space. In this moment the world as I knew it had stopped. I felt warmly enveloped in and infused with clarity and well-being.

As this transcendent experience unfolded, I was perfectly aware of riding a test and that my horse was beneath me. Foley and I were so attuned to each other that a thought was all I needed to guide him. Completely relaxed and happy, I approached the end of the diagonal. The enlightening aura that had surrounded me receded, and I proceeded with the remainder of the test.

I had never experienced anything like this. The fact that it occurred when I was on Foley, in the middle of a dressage test, made the event all the more meaningful. What had just happened? And why? And why at that particular time?

Perhaps I'll never know the answers to these questions, but those mystical moments during the dressage test were ones I will always treasure and embrace with the deepest regard. For me they provided an awe-filled awakening — a gift and a glimpse into an unknown place. I will be forever grateful that I was touched this way while being with Foley and doing something I love so dearly.

On my test, the judge's comment about our trip across the diagonal was "lovely freedom," and she gave us a score of eight.

That is exactly what it was — a lovely freedom. If the judge had had an inkling of what was happening invisibly during those few moments, I do believe she would have happily given us a ten. And to top it off, we placed first in our Second Level 4 test.

On September 19, 2005, I had to say a final good-bye to my beautiful horse, Foley. For over twenty-five years he had been my friend and my teacher. He served as my steady guide to learning more about not only horsemanship and dressage but also truly loving and being with horses. He showed me the way toward truth and honesty in my riding. He patiently waited for me to figure things out as I made my way from one mistake to the next with bits of progress sprinkled throughout. He was there for me every day of his life. His generosity and kindness of heart were an inspiration to me, and I will always miss him.

Misty, thank you for being my best friend and confidante. Your kind soul and complete faith in me led me to a life filled with remarkable horses, and the people whom they loved. Foley, thank you for an incredible education and friendship. Your love and trust guided me in all we did together. You are the essence and spirit of Muzzey Hill Farm.

Meditation

Have you ever had a transcendent experience while in the presence of a horse or when you were doing something you love deeply? Would writing about it help you to appreciate the moment more?

Abby's Secret Life

Kris Bowman
Newport, Pennsylvania

I've been talking to horses since I was very small. Back then I thought everyone could do this. I would get messages from horses in images, emotions, thoughts, and sometimes clear statements. The first time it happened I was around four or five years old. While at a county fair with my parents, I watched a small pony giving rides. He let me know his back hurt badly from a saddle.

When I became a teenager I realized that not everyone could get thoughts from their horses and that some people viewed me as strange because I could. Every time I tried to tell someone that a horse was in pain or feeling sad, that person would ask where I had gotten my information. People would tell me to just keep it to myself, as they didn't believe horses talked. Being a shy, quiet child, I was embarrassed and quickly learned to stay silent.

As an adult I have used the ability to communicate with horses in my wonderful career teaching horses and humans to get along better. Communication helps me understand why a horse is behaving as he does or is acting foolish around a certain person. It is normal for me to be carrying on a conversation with a horse while I am listening to the owner's troubles.

For instance, one time I visited a horse stable to give a riding lesson to two little girls. Their mother had called to tell me that their two equines had taken over as bosses, and she was afraid that one of her daughters would get hurt riding them. That day, as I walked to their riding ring, the Arabian horse looked at me and all but said, "Well, it is about time you got here." It seemed the little girls had been taught incorrectly how to place the horses' saddles. That poor Arabian horse was in pain. He knew I had come to help him.

One time I felt a strong mental pull toward my barn. It was almost bedtime, and I didn't feel like taking that trudge to the barn, but I did. My favorite mare, Lynn, was asking me to come to her.

When I arrived at the barn I found Lynn down in her stall. She had gotten her hind hoof caught in her stable blanket strap. She was unable to get up without hurting herself or tearing her nice new blanket. I unfastened the strap, and she got up, thanking me for the help. I rubbed her forehead and then walked back to the house.

I've raised and trained Percheron horses for about fifteen years. The Percheron is a draft horse originating in France. The breed was first used as a French knight's warhorse, then as a beast of burden to move heavy loads in the cities and for plowing fields in the country-side. Percherons are big horses, ranging in size from 16 to over 19 hands tall at their shoulders (withers). The Percheron horse is now popular with taller riders and for driving a wheeled vehicle. We show our horses in hitching classes with other Percherons, and I compete against the light breeds — Morgans, Arabians, and so forth — in pleasure shows. I love these horses because of their grand temperaments and intelligence. They are kind, love working with their people, and enjoy being a part of the family.

One year my husband, Glenn, told me that for my Christmas

gift he wanted to take me to a draft horse sale. He said that from all the draft horses being offered, I could pick a very special gift on four legs — a show filly. After going through a divorce some years before, I had stopped showing these wonderful animals since it just was no fun anymore. So my wonderful, supportive new husband figured he'd give me a horse to work with because he knew that showing horses had once been an important part of my life.

I pored over the sales catalog and studied each mare's bloodlines, heights, and show careers. Finally I settled on four possible horses. On the morning of the sale we headed out bright and early. By lunchtime I'd decided I wanted to see two horses. I liked one, but my husband really liked another, a two-year-old filly. When bidding was over, we owned both of them.

One of the fillies, Betsy, settled into her new home easily. However, Abby, the one I'd chosen, seemed aloof, and I didn't know why.

I started by calling the horse Fashion, as this was part of her registered name, Wolf River Fashion. Right away she told me, "I am not Fashion. I am Abby."

Abby was going to turn two years old that April, so she was very young. She is pure black with only a few white hairs on her forehead. Fully grown, she is 17 hands tall.

Abby was never nasty or grumpy, always the model filly, yet it seemed that she wasn't happy and didn't like it here very much. She moped around and wouldn't respond when I scratched her, something that most horses love. She seemed so alone, even when in the midst of other horses.

One day that first month, as I was cleaning Abby's stall, I noticed her trying to pick up my rake by its handle. I stopped and watched, smiling at her antics. Suddenly she stood ever so still and looked into my eyes. She told me that she was confused and communicated questions: What happened? Where was her other human? And did I know that she had been a mom before this?

What? I thought. Abby had just turned two. There was no way she could have had a foal. Yet I was fascinated, as she began sending me pictures of long, open grassy meadows with white fencing around them in the distance. She showed me that there were other horses in this place and they were not draft horses. They were her friends, though. Then I got a clear image of a small black foal. I knew she was trying to let me know that it had been *her* foal. Abby told me that she had lived with other broodmares and was very happy in this place. I also learned how sad she was to leave that life. Then the images were gone.

Abby stepped over to me, put her massive head on my shoulder, and gave a big sigh. She told me that she would be happy to live here now and was relieved that I hadn't blocked her past. I felt tears come to my eyes. Abby had finally let me into her heart. What a huge compliment that was! Sniffling, I hugged her. Then it was back to stall cleaning for me and hay munching for Abby. Later I told my husband about this. He was pleased to hear about the breakthrough with my lovely mare.

Ever since that day when Abby told me her secrets, she has continued to send me thoughts and ideas. I learned that she felt like she was being passed on from person to person without having a chance to really settle in anywhere. She recently told me that she was ready to do "things." I had to think about what she meant by "things." Then I discovered that Abby felt she was ready to move forward in her harness training.

We'd had to put her harness training on hold for a year because she would cringe in fear whenever I tried to harness her or would get confused, rearing up in harness. Clearly she'd received bad training with the owner who had brought her to the sale and this had left her frightened. She did not want a bit in her mouth and let me know quickly that I was using the wrong kind.

When I tried to ground drive, walking behind Abby with long lines to teach her to turn or stop, she would not listen to my soft signals on the lines. This is basic training for many young horses to start them correctly. Her fear was a result of not being treated kindly. Someone had just thrown a harness on her, rushing her into being driven long before she understood it all. Because of her panic, she learned to misbehave and would try to run away from being harnessed. She wanted nothing to do with wheeled vehicles.

I had given her a year off of harness training so she could mature. Apparently it had worked. This year, after she told me she was ready, she was much happier and tried her best not to show fear. I used a different bit, one that she loved, and all was good again. This time, my Abby would turn with a soft tug on her driving lines, stop, and stand patiently for me to ask her to walk on, waiting with her ears pointed back toward my voice. What a good girl she was growing up to be! She was interested in sniffing the cart all over, even shoving the wheel some with her nose.

Abby's success in harness training came about because I listened for when she told me she was ready.

Today Abby is a well-mannered five-year-old mare. She loves me and shows it by giving me nuzzles, talking to me, and whinnying when I come to the barn. She's very vocal at feeding times, where before she was silent. She sees me as Abby's Person and always comes when called, even when it means leaving her favorite grazing areas. If she had not tried to tell me how she was feeling that day in the barn, I may never have realized why this wonderful horse was so sad.

I am her human, and she is my mare. Abby will live with us for the rest of her life here on earth.

Meditation

Is there a horse or other animal who is trying to tell you a secret that would help you understand? Are you listening and receptive to the communication?

Ginny Goes Home to Her Horses

Margaret Nordeen
Chico, California

*I*n mid-February 2002 my sister Ginny was losing her battle with cancer. Hospitalized for the third time, she began pleading with everyone to be allowed to return home. The doctors still held on to a strand of hope and worried that if her treatment were interrupted she would die, so Ginny remained at the hospital.

Ginny longed for her home, fifty miles outside of Anchorage, where she and her husband had built their humble two-story abode on a lake, deep in the woods, surrounded by snowy mountains. Years earlier she had fought developers to protect the loons on this lake. It had been a long, arduous struggle, but finally, after years of city council meetings and numerous letters, she and a small group of neighbors had won. She yearned to see the loons' sanctuary for the last time. Most of all, she wanted to say good-bye to her beloved horses, Raspberry, Cinnamon, and Rose.

As a young girl Ginny had spent many hours riding and hanging out at the stables in northern Minnesota where our family lived. "Someday I'm going to move to Kansas and raise horses," she would say.

But after we moved away from Minnesota in 1963, Ginny's interest and love for horses disappeared, only to resurface thirty years later. As if she had rediscovered gold, her phone calls to me in California were filled with enthusiasm and excitement. She described in intricate detail the training, riding, and feeding of her three new horses. One day she said, "Maggie, Cinnamon was hurt in the past, so I have to reassure her that no one will ever mistreat her again." Ginny was always compassionate and patient yet firm. On several occasions I watched as she worked with the horses. It was enjoyable to observe her always praising them by saying, "You've come a long way, baby!" In response they would affectionately nudge her.

I remember thinking later, after she was gone, if only Ginny had worked with horses instead of having a desk job, she'd still be alive today. Horses were always her true calling.

After Ginny died at the end of February, my husband and I gathered with others for Ginny's funeral in the home of her closest friend, Linda. We were quietly chatting when a strong outdoors-type woman approached me. She had been taking care of the place while Ginny's husband, Rege, stayed at the hospital, only returning home long enough to shower and change clothes.

This redheaded woman whispered, "You know, it was the strangest thing. For several nights before she died, we heard all this commotion at your sister's place. My husband and I worried that intruders were trying to break in. We would go over there with flashlights, but everything would be quiet, except for the horses. They were restless, stirring, jumping up and plunging down."

I looked at the woman's face as she described the scene. *Horses jumping, as if someone was there?*

She continued, "It was scary at first. But then it continued for three

Ginny and her horse in the snow

nights in a row. The horses were making the same type of commotion as when they saw your sister coming to see them. After Ginny died, the horses stopped acting that way."

The woman studied my face as if to see whether I understood what she was *really* saying. I looked into her dark green eyes and said, "That doesn't surprise me about Ginny." I let out a long, deep sigh. "She begged the hospital staff to let her go. Looks as though she found her own way. She loved those horses and wanted to die at home."

My eyes filled with tears. The woman nodded in agreement and said, "Well, that's what we thought, but we didn't want to say it. People would think we were crazy."

I smiled through my tears and said, "Thank you for sharing this story."

The woman squeezed my hand and said, "We loved Ginny. She was an animal lover if there ever was one."

It seems that life and death intertwine in a mystery that we can't always comprehend. In yet another mysterious twist, one of Ginny's horses, Rose, passed away only one month after my sister died. It was as if Rose couldn't live without her friend, Ginny.

My sister had experienced many hardships in her adult life. Horses helped her regain the joy she once knew as a child and enabled a return to her true nature. They had also aided in Ginny's healing and long struggle with illness. In return, all she wanted was to say good-bye to them.

Meditation

What horses will be with you as you near death? Do you believe that love will transcend death?

Playing Games with My Pal, Brady

By Sam Younghans
Huntington Beach, California

*M*y daughter, Candace, was taking riding lessons at a ranch outside San Marcos, California. One day a truck delivered a horse to the ranch for a woman who was also taking lessons. Before making a purchase, she wanted to ride Brady, a thoroughbred of about 17 hands. The woman decided Brady was too much horse for her, so the trainer at the ranch asked Candace to ride him. It was love at first sight. That same day we bought Brady. Candace and Brady immediately became a team, with Candace spending most of her free time riding the horse.

After she graduated from high school, Candace worked for a year to save money for a six-month backpacking trip to Europe with our neighbor's daughter. Candace insisted that I take riding lessons so I could exercise Brady while she was away. Although I had been riding horses most of my life, I looked forward to a little English training and some jumping. This would be a new, interesting experience.

After our exercise Brady and I played a simple game. I moved him to the end of the arena, and then I went to the middle, holding a lunging whip. I'd say, "Okay, Brady," and he would immediately try to get past me. I never hit him with the whip, just cracked it in front to turn him. We had fun, and after a few attempts he always managed to get past me. The people at the ranch, laughing, thought I was nuts. Nobody played games with a horse. Horses are for riding. I may be nuts, but this is one of the ways that Brady and I bonded.

When Candace returned from Europe, she moved to San Francisco to attend school. We decided to bring Brady to our home from the ranch where he had been stabled and place him in a pipe corral that we set up next to the house.

Our house sat on a knoll between two neighbors. In front of the property was a large field, bordered by trees, that sloped down into a small valley. The driveway was open, and we shared a dirt road that led to a paved street below. We left the corral gate open most of the time, leaving Brady free to roam. We only closed it if we knew we would be gone for a couple of hours or more. Brady never walked off our land alone, and he no longer wore a halter.

By this time Brady was one of the family. When I drove into the yard, Brady was there to greet me. He'd walk up to the car, and if I had my window down he'd stick his head into the car and nuzzle me. This washed away all the problems of the day.

After Brady came to live with us, he and I continued to invent more games. All I needed to say was, "Brady, let's go for a walk." He would instantly be ready for us to walk down the dirt road to the mailbox at its bottom. Then we walked into the field below the road and back home. Other times we went through a stand of trees and down the slope to a valley below, with Brady following me through the trees. Once we passed the trees, it was playtime. Brady would dash past me and run halfway down the hill to an area where he liked to roll. He loved to roll.

When I walked past him, continuing down the hill, it was his signal to get up and bound past me, each time pretending he was going to run over me. I would stand my ground, and at the last minute he'd swerve. Once he reached the bottom of the hill, he had another favorite spot where he liked to roll. When he finished rolling, I would shout, "Go, Brady." And away he'd race, up and down the valley at a full gallop.

After a few fast sprints, I'd say, "Let's go for a walk, Brady." This was the signal for us to climb between rocks and trees and up the other side of the valley, with Brady following me like a puppy. If he lagged, chewing on some tender morsels of grass, I'd hide behind a bush. When he noticed I was gone, he'd dash up and down the hill and around the bush, pretending to look for me. It was our way of playing hide-and-seek.

At the bottom of the hill there were three or four large pepper trees. Their limbs hung over and formed a large tent. While I hid in the trees, Brady ran around them, looking for me. After he finished searching, I'd come out of the trees on the downside of the hill. When he spotted me, he'd gallop over. Sometimes he'd rear up in front of me. I always applauded him when he did this. Then he usually went to the bottom of the hill for another roll.

After our walk we would play one final game: Who gets back to the top of the hill first? I'd wait until he was rolling in one of his favorite spots in the valley. While he was occupied, I'd quietly move back under the trees. Then I'd dart out from the other side, running up the hill as fast as I could, trying to reach a small stand of trees and big boulders near the top. That was our home base. He'd stop rolling, jump up from the ground, and gallop around the trees and up the hill, trying to beat me to our home base at the top. He usually won. If I won he would act rather dejected. But when he won he was king of the hill.

Our games over, I'd say, "Let's go home, Brady." He would simply turn to the path and start for home. Sometimes we walked side by side; other times he led or I led. It never mattered because we both knew where we were going. Back on our property, Brady headed for his corral while I went to the hay barn to get his ration of hay. If I started toward the house instead of the hay barn, Brady would cut me off, forcing me to go to the barn to get his hay.

One time I had an idea for a funny skit with Brady. My daughter, Candace, videotaped it.

I was standing on a stool, working under the hood of an old pickup truck. The script called for Brady to walk over and bite me in the rear while I bent over the engine. The first couple of times, he just stuck his head under the hood to see what I was doing. My daughter said, "Give him a wrench, Dad, he wants to help."

Candace and Brady

Brady loved carrots, so I stuck one in my hip pocket and began to work. He started nuzzling my pocket for the carrot. I stuck my foot out to push him away. He grabbed my foot and pulled me off the stool. The tools and I went crashing to the ground. Like a naughty child, Brady bounded away but returned to see what had happened. He stood over me as if to say, "What are you doing down there?"

Brady and I communicated in ways that I've never experienced with a person. It was as if we were one. He knew what I was thinking, and I knew what he was thinking. For example, he always knew when we were going for those walks. If I even thought about walking, he would stand by the front door waiting for me. If I came out and just stood there instead of opening the door, he pushed me with his nose. Also, I always had to pass through the trees before he would follow me instead of running ahead. Only after I passed the trees would he think it was okay for him to run down the hill and start our games.

As I write this story, the memories are so strong that many times I have to sit back, relive them, and feel that love again. Thank you, Brady.

Meditation

How has having a spiritual connection and inner communication with a horse brought more joy into your life?

Living with the Mare Goddess, Chinamoon

Flash Silvermoon
Melrose, Florida

*O*n my forty-ninth birthday, I decided to change my life by changing my location. I had recently learned that my solar return (the astrological chart of a person's coming year as seen through the lens of the birthday for that year) had great aspects but that they were locked up in the twelfth house of hidden energies. Being one who likes to maximize the positive as well as seek adventure, I scoped out where I would physically have to be on March 18, 1999, in order to bring all those locked-up energies into the first house, where I could use them more easily. Surprisingly, Los Angeles was the place for me to visit.

Not typically finding that town to my liking, I wondered what type of new madness I was contemplating. I did have a few friends there. They offered to house my partner, Tara, and me for the week. So we bought tickets and flew to Los Angeles.

Part of what I am trying to get across here is the fact that before this, I was a pretty laid-back kind of woman who does not make major changes on whim or impulse. All this was about to change as I gained access to my hidden energies.

The trip did activate the strong, go-for-it energies that I had hoped it would. Back at home, while putting up a flyer for one of my animal communication workshops, I spied an index card on the veterinarian's bulletin board saying, "Appaloosa Mare For Sale." I felt compelled to call the owner immediately.

Tara had told me, "No more big dogs for a while!" Just below the horse-for-sale card was a picture of a beautiful German shepherd, advertised as free to a good home. The dog's nose pointed mystically toward the "Appaloosa Mare For Sale" card, which described the horse as "A real yard puppy. Loves water."

My heart was beating a million miles per minute. *I must see this horse*, I thought and hastily called Tara to ask her to go with me. After all, this Appaloosa was not a large dog.

I found out later that it was good that I had hurried, for many people came after me and wanted the horse called China. I drove like a speed demon to Heidi's house, where China was living. Heidi and her husband were moving to Idaho and needed to sell all their horses.

When I first laid eyes on China, I thought I had found heaven on earth. There she was, a beautiful, dark five-year-old Appaloosa mare, with expressive brown eyes that could pierce your very soul. A mostly brown mare, she had what is called a double blanket, that is, many white spots on her dark rump mixed with a few lighter brown blotches.

China proceeded to lick me all over as if I were her favorite Popsicle. I asked, "Is she always like this?"

Heidi said, "Yeah, she's friendly, but this is a bit much, even for her. I think she's chosen her new person."

I was in love. As I stroked the horse's chest and looked into her eyes, I could hear China whispering inside my head and heart, "Don't you remember me?" I almost broke into tears. I knew that China was the reincarnation of my beloved German shepherd, Moonshadow.

"Yes, I remember you," I whispered back as China continued to lick my face.

I began stroking China's third eye (the center of her forehead). She loved it and went into a trance for at least ten minutes, not moving even a hair. I interrupted the mystical moment by stroking her neck, and she released every one of her neck muscles in a movement that was poetry in motion.

Seconds later, China began circling my feet. Round and round she strolled, looking for that perfect spot. Then she lay down, forming a semicircle around my legs and putting her head on top of my foot. By this time Heidi was panicking and asked, "Oh no! Is she sick?"

"Nah," I told her, "she's just showing us who she is. That's all."

When Moonshadow was winding down her life, she was afflicted by seizures. I had often spent an hour at a time with my foot under her head to protect her from injuring herself on the ground.

Since that first day at Heidi's house, China has never repeated the performance of placing her head on my foot. It was no longer necessary. I had gotten the message that she had returned. Moonshadow was back, bigger and more awesome than ever. We all had to agree: China was no ordinary horse.

After China let me know that she carried Moonshadow's spirit, I gave Heidi a five-hundred-dollar deposit for the horse, much to Tara's, and even my, shock. After nearly seven years, I have never regretted that decisive moment.

It took a lot of time, effort, and money to ready my home, Moonhaven, for China, whose name on her papers was Seekers China Doll. Clearly her name needed to reflect her new identity. So she became Chinamoon. The name symbolized that the mare had started this life as China but now carried the Moon in her heart too.

I wasn't able to see much of China in those torturous weeks of waiting and prepping Moonhaven. When I first brought China home, I was concerned about intro-

Flash's Chinamoon

ducing her onto the land, to her pasture and barn. New surroundings can sometimes spook a horse. No need to worry, though. When I began to walk China onto the land from the trailer, she strolled in like she owned the place, because she did, and she never looked back. Chinamoon had come home.

And that was just the beginning.

After Chinamoon joined us, Tara and I worked on her auric field as she went through the process of healing from West Nile virus. Her auric field felt quite strong and vibrated some four feet from her body. When I rechecked her flower essences, I had the clearest understanding about her vulnerability to West Nile. I dowsed with my faithful pendulum over many boxes of flower essences before discovering that Chinamoon needed Grief and Loss in the special mix for her grid. (A grid is a miniature healing temple of the animal or person, created with stones, symbols, flower essences, or other healing items.)

Chinamoon had been suffering, as I had, over the loss of our kittens, Manuelo and Serena. They were buried near her stall. The kittens used to play with Chinamoon in the pasture like little gray bolts of light and joy, dancing across the sand of her paddock. In my mind I could hear Chinamoon blaming herself for not being a good enough protector, for letting the kittens slip through somehow — on her watch. It became clear that she was punishing herself emotionally. Her grief had been palpable at Serena's funeral, as she stood next to me with her head bowed.

Besides using the flower essences to help her heal, Tara and I figured out a way for Chinamoon to be more included in the home life of Moonhaven. It's always nice to be closer to your mom when you don't feel well. And Chinamoon was still grieving for Manuelo and Serena. So we took a screen off one of the windows in the computer room. Now Chinamoon could put her whole head inside if she wanted.

I was reminded, as we opened the window for her, how much she is a creature of habit. It took continual coaxing with carrots and bananas to get her to believe that the glass was really gone, not just well cleaned. We played with her muzzle and blew her breathy kisses. Chinamoon snuffled back, kissing the top of my head. It was comical to watch her, still in disbelief that she could possibly have her head on mine when I was inside the house and she outside it.

As Chinamoon stared at me intensely but lovingly through the office window while I sat at my computer, I felt that it was finally time to write her story. And who better to supervise than the Grand Dam — or should I say the Goddess Mare Herself?

Meditation

Do you see the eyes of a familiar old soul when you look into the eyes of a horse who loves you?

Grace

Jane Larson Wipf
Minneapolis, Minnesota

*O*ne summer I visited a farm for two days to take part in a workshop dealing with horses and intuition. Twelve women attended the meeting, all of them having some connection with horses, either because they had a horse or felt at home with them. I was there because I was afraid of falling off of or being hurt by a horse. I viewed horses as big, powerful, and unpredictable.

At the beginning, while being instructed in horse safety, we only observed the horses. My heart was beating so hard it felt like it would escape my chest. Later we were asked to choose a horse to work with. As I roamed the corral and barn, large horses — Arabian, pinto, thoroughbred — surrounded me. Feeling fearful, I decided that a small horse might be easier for me to work with.

My eyes were drawn to two large brown thoroughbreds in the corral. Glad that a fence separated us, I stood and watched them. Their muscles rippled in the sun. Both horses looked so strong and alive, they were captivating my spirit. As I tried to choose between them, one in particular stared fixedly at me for a long time. I felt fearful yet excited. Our instructor had told us, "The horse may choose *you*." I felt cornered by the alert presence of this horse, whose penetrating eyes seemed, for a moment, intimidating. I thought that she knew I was afraid.

Each horse wore a rune symbol on his or her backside. The other women and I sat down to decipher the symbol that correlated with the name of the horse we had paired up with. My horse turned out to be a mare with the name of Grace. She was a tall, shiny brown beauty whose rune symbol linked with the word *openings*. That meaning, along with her name, fit how I wanted to embrace this workshop — to be open. And I liked it that Grace and I were both females.

One by one, each of us went into the barn corral to be alone with her horse. The first minutes I spent by myself with Grace, she wanted nothing to do with me. I took it personally. Not only was I terrified of this horse, but she had rejected me.

My instructor said that maybe Grace didn't want contact with me then since she was eating. *My* time was not *her* timing. Maybe so, like God, whose timing is always perfect.

The second day I tried to remain upbeat. Our assignment for that day was to try to engage in a dance with our horse. Watching others interact with their horses had helped to put me at ease. I thought, *Okay, I can try that!*

Instinctively I took off my jacket and removed my watch to start anew, to be open and bold. Praying as I stepped into the corral, trusting as if I were a child, helped to calm my racing heart. This would be the last time that I could be alone with Grace. I wanted to get to know her and overcome my fears. I wanted desperately for her to accept me.

One of the instructors told me to approach Grace in a manner that showed I was a leader by throwing back my shoulders and exhaling. I petted Grace firmly above her shoulder, inviting her to come and follow to the left. Nothing I did worked. She wouldn't move. Then I tried walking to the right. She followed only partway. Stubborn lady!

Feeling like giving up, I went to an opening in the corral barn and stood at the fence, deeply breathing the fresh air, in and out, with my eyes skyward. My time with Grace was almost up. I walked back to this giant creature and stroked her again with both hands.

Without warning, Grace's front legs folded as if in slow motion amid a cloud of dust. Then she folded her back two legs until she sat on all fours on the ground. Suddenly she looked so small. I was overwhelmed with emotion and surprise. My instinct was to fall on my knees beside Grace, so I did.

Her nose became relaxed, touching the ground. She sat still, and I touched her. Never in my life have I felt so anchored, peaceful, and still. By placing her trust in me, Grace had the power to quiet my heart and heal it.

As suddenly as she had folded to the ground, Grace turned on her back for a few moments with all four legs up in the air, looking vulnerable as could be. Then she rolled and got up.

Afterward I continued to feel at peace and sensed that my heart had opened. I felt reassured of my trustworthiness. I believe Grace made herself as small as she could in size and stillness so that my fears could dissolve into pure love and respect for the beautiful creature she is. I had fallen into the stillness of God's presence. Oh, the great gift Grace gives!

Meditation

When has a horse intuited your secret wishes and given you exactly what you needed?

Benni Teaches Me to Trust in God

Laura Steidl
Weyauwega, Wisconsin

$\mathcal{T}$he truck is filled with everything necessary for a horseback riding adventure. The horse trailer is ready for Benni, my mighty steed, who will ride in it to Hartman Creek State Park. I only have to hook the truck and trailer together and load the horse.

Benni is a beautiful, gray four-year-old crossbred gelding. He is registered as a Gaited Spanish Pleasure Horse and a Gaited Baroque Horse. His sire is a Gaited Mustang, and his dam is a Peruvian Paso. Benni grew up in Colorado for three years until I brought him home to Wisconsin. I found him through the Internet horse support group that I joined after my Peruvian Paso died. I needed help grieving this loss. The fact that Benni was placed in my life without me actively searching for him convinced me that God has put him here for a reason.

Just a few hours before taking our trip today, I brushed Benni until he sparkled, but now he is caked with black swamp muck. He needs a bath before any saddle of mine will be allowed to touch him.

Not a problem. The quick bath goes smoothly, and I still have time to spare before we are to meet up with our riding buddies at the park. However, I really should hook the trailer to the truck before the bath, because I can't load Benni until I do. He can't go back out in that dirty pasture because he will roll — again. The only other choice is to put him in his stall.

This horse always hates being in a stall. Whenever I put him in it, he stands and bangs the stall door with his front foot, only stopping to paw like a maniac for a brief change of pace. Then he resumes banging on the door. But I have been working with him, using positive reinforcement to reward those rare moments when he stands quietly. So I tell myself that he will be fine for three to five minutes while I hook the trailer to the truck.

Into the stall he goes. I tell him to be quiet and I'll be right back.

I go to the barn to get my truck. As I am backing it out, I don't hear one bang on the stall door. Pleasure is written all over my face — until I see my horse on his back legs, trying to climb over the side wall of the stall. I reassure him by calling out, "It's all right, Benni, I'll be right back."

That gets his attention. He climbs down and comes to the front of the stall. But something tells me to get him out of there and put him in the pasture before he causes a wreck.

I am too late. He rears up and slams his front hooves against the boards high up at the front of the stall. This stall was built with green lumber — white oak boards that shrank after they cured, leaving small gaps everywhere. On the front wall, where the sliding door rail is attached at the top, is a small space between two-by-six-inch boards. The space has become bigger over time and is more than seven and a half feet from the floor. When I reach the stall to get Benni out, his right front hoof has wedged into that space and is hanging there.

I carry a sturdy metal bench, which I normally can barely move, over to the stall. I can climb up on it to reach the hoof by which my horse is now hanging. The hoof won't budge from the tight little crevice. I try to break the white oak board with a crowbar, but it seems that the more I struggle to free Benni, the more he twists and turns. I fear that his leg will break.

I go to the house and call 911.

"So sorry, but that's not our kind of emergency. Call a veterinarian," they say.

I plead with them to send someone who can get my horse down. My neighbors are all away. My husband is not home. Our regular vet is too far away. But they don't care.

The closest equine vet clinic is twenty-five miles away. I call there and am told that a vet could do nothing to get my horse down. They will be happy to come to my place and treat his injuries after someone else gets him down. Should they list mine as a call for veterinary service?

"No!" I say and hang up.

Then I call Great Lakes Veterinary Clinic in Neehah, Wisconsin. They say they will get in touch with the horse vet, Dr. Fox, and have her call me right back.

I think of a friend from days gone by who raises saddlebreds and lives ten miles away. I call them, and thankfully she and her husband are both home. They say, "We'll be right there!"

In the meantime, the clinic calls to say they are still trying to get in touch with the vet. They also ask questions about the condition of the horse and want directions to my place.

Benni seems to be fading. His foot is still stuck as tight as ever. His breathing has become weak and erratic. I feel so helpless.

As I try different things to get him free and call other people, I keep asking God to show me the way to get that hoof free. *Just plant the idea in my head, so I can do it,* I pray.

Now Benni has been hanging by his foot for over thirty minutes. Nothing I have tried even comes close to freeing him. I figure that by the time my friends or the vet arrive, Benni will be dead, and I will be hysterical.

Then it comes to me. *I* am not meant to save my horse, *God* is.

I close my eyes and pray for a miracle. I tell God that I just can't do it and I am afraid my horse will die before someone comes to help us. So would he please free Benni's foot?

While I pray I stand in the doorway of the barn, facing out. My eyes are closed. I have the image in my mind of God's hand reaching down from heaven in a beam of light and touching Benni's shoulder. In my thoughts God holds his hand there to relax Benni and soften the hoof that is wedged. It then easily slips free. Oddly, my body relaxes as I visualize this scene. My heart opens, and I feel a sense of inner peace while I relinquish control to God. It is such a relief to completely trust him.

When I finish praying I hear a noise and turn to look at the stall. Benni's foot is free. He is standing on all four legs in his stall. God has answered my prayer and given me a miracle.

Two minutes later my friends arrive. Fifteen minutes after that, Dr. Fox is here. By now Benni is going into shock, and his muscles have tied up. Sweat pours from his whole body. He is clearly in excruciating pain. His whole body has been affected by massive contractions of the muscles, with the back and rump being the most afflicted.

Muscle cells have already started to die because blood flow was poor during his fierce muscle contractions. Dr. Fox explains that as the muscle cells die, they release a substance called myoglobin into the bloodstream. Myoglobin is cleared from the blood via the kidneys. If there is too much of it, the kidneys can shut down and the horse will die. That is the bad news. The good news is that nothing was broken and nothing appears to be torn.

Treatment has to begin immediately. First, treat the pain. Next, dilate the blood vessels for better circulation so more muscle cells don't die. Dr. Fox gives Benni another drug to stabilize the muscle cell walls, which also helps to limit the number of muscle cells that will die. Finally, Benni gets a muscle-relaxing drug.

Dr. Fox wraps all four of Benni's legs for support. She says that Benni needs to stay in a stall for three to five days to rest his muscles. My friend reminds the vet that my horse won't stay quietly in a stall for three to five minutes. How does she think I can keep Benni there for three to five days?

Dr. Fox tells me to try, so I do.

After only four hours in the stall, with constant supervision, I must put

Laura and Benni

Benni outside for his own protection. Using instinct and common sense, he quietly stands in his run-in shelter and rests his muscles like a good boy.

Before the vet leaves, she takes a huge vile of blood for testing the amount of myoglobin in Benni's blood. If the horse has too much, he will have to go immediately to the clinic and receive twelve to twenty liters of intravenous fluids to dilute the concentration of myoglobin and save the kidneys by flushing them. His myoglobin count is only moderately elevated, so Dr. Fox decides that I do not have to take Benni to the clinic for intravenous treatment.

Happily Benni recovers completely. He is living proof that miracles do happen. He has helped me to learn a valuable lesson: Stop being so arrogant in thinking I should always be in charge and do everything myself. God was more than happy to save my horse; I just needed to ask him for help.

My natural instinct is to be a leader who is in charge. Asking for help is hard, but I have had to learn to do this with people as well as with God. In this situation I had to surrender and trust God to take complete control. I am a better person because of it. For a long time God has been trying to teach me about trust. In fact, I can see him smile and give a big sigh of relief because I finally got it.

God knows that I connect with animals much easier than I do with people. Animals open my heart and mind. With them, I am able to gain more perspective than when I am with people.

Benni was brought into my life to further my spiritual education. My experience with Benni teaches me to let go, open my heart, and trust God to control my life. Benni is young. What will my next lessons be with him as God's instrument?

Meditation

Has an experience with a horse or other animal turned miraculous when you surrendered your will and turned the situation over to a Higher Power?

Five Star Winner

Maureen Sinisi
Township of Washington, New Jersey

One day I visited a farm in Blairstown, New Jersey, where my brother-in-law kept his retired racehorses. I wanted to take care of the horses and to have a new experience with these fine beings. Years earlier, I had had an inner spiritual experience with Pegasus, the winged horse of the gods in Greek mythology. It came at a time when I was troubled in my life and marriage and needed to have more love. Since the experience with Pegasus, I had always wanted to learn more about the divinity in horses.

When I arrived at my brother-in-law's farm, I went into the barn where the horses were stalled. I was filled with love when I entered into Five Star Winner's stall. This horse stood 16.5 hands high and was solid muscle. He was a brown thoroughbred with a white stripe down the front of his nose and two white boots on his back legs. He lived up to his name as a star because he had made a lot of money for the family. Everything with thoroughbred racehorses has to do with bloodline. Five Star Winner came from royalty. His bloodline was that of Bold Runner, one of the top horses in racing history.

Having to retire to a barn where he was cooped up after living in the limelight as a superstar made Five Star Winner often moody. Being a thoroughbred, he was high-strung.

That day I proceeded to lovingly brush and groom him while practicing the presence of Divine Spirit. I do spiritual exercises and try to live my life guided by love, so I chanted "HU," an ancient love song to God. My sole intention was to give this horse as much divine love as I could muster.

Five Star Winner graciously tolerated me, sometimes looking around and moving. I began cleaning the bedding in his stall, giving him fresh water, and doing chores to make his living space more enjoyable.

Five Star Winner

Five Star Winner's reaction to me in his stall was one of wonder and curiosity. He must have sensed that I had only love to give. I respected this wonderful being, and he knew it. I talked with him, telling him that I loved him. He would turn and look at me. As atoms of light and sound surrounded and blessed me, I shared the love with him.

After taking care of Five Star, I went to the brood mares. I gave all of them unconditional love too. I treated each horse with special attention as an individual, unique being.

Later my brother-in-law drove up to the farm and asked how I was doing. I said that I was fine and had introduced myself to all the horses. I had also groomed Five Star Winner and taken care of his stall. My brother-in-law reacted with shock. He shook his head as if he thought I was crazy. "You did what? That horse is mean. He doesn't like anybody. You're lucky that you didn't get hurt."

I just smiled and said, "That horse loves me. He wouldn't hurt me. He needed the love I gave to him. He and I are bonded now."

I knew that it was the protection and love of the Holy Spirit that had allowed me to connect spiritually with Five Star Winner. This being, like all of God's creatures, knows love when he sees it and responds in kind. Five Star Winner was proof that love sustains us all. Every creature is a divine being who needs to give and receive love. Love knows no boundaries. Love is what we live for.

Meditation

Would you like to fill your heart with love and chant "HU" (pronounced *hue*), the ancient love song to God, while you are with a horse or other animal?

Pegasus in Disguise

Renee van Asten
Santa Fe, New Mexico

*M*y arms were folded around his head and across his chest. He lifted up his head to look at the monitors and noticed his heartbeat had slowed down to thirty-four. "I am almost there," he said. I stared blankly at the number and at him, not able to think. Then, a few seconds later, he took his last breath. My most treasured husband was gone.

Returning home, still blank, still incapable of thought, I had gone numb. I had died along with him.

I parked my truck near my house, then stumbled out and dragged myself over to the nearest corral. The moon was at its fullest. In its white light I saw my horse Comanche standing still, not moving a muscle or a hair of his silver mane. His white coat had a bluish sheen. His tail draped to the floor like a silver waterfall. It looked as if he was not even breathing.

The epitome of the magnificent white stallion, depicted in so many paintings, Comanche had a muscular, broad-chested frame that belied his 15 hands. Most people guessed his heritage to be Andalusian, that magnificent Spanish breed. Yet he was part quarter horse, part carriage horse, part Welsh pony, and the rest Arabian. With his huge eyes set above broad jaws, he made an impact of immense proportions wherever he went. People always gawked at him admiringly.

I put both of my arms over the top rail of the corral, hanging on to steady my now-weak legs. Devastation washed over me. I thought I would faint. My eyes riveted upon Comanche as I tried to make sure I was still alive and that he was real.

The two of us stood motionless for some time. Then Comanche suddenly moved. He reared up. While holding himself airborne, he stepped to the right, on and on and on, turning a complete circle before bringing his front legs back down to the ground. All the while, he shook his magnificent mane to the left and to the right. Dipping his broad neck to the ground, he gathered his strength and reared up again. Dancing in a circle and weaving his neck, once again, he shook his silver mane.

His mouth was slightly open, and it looked like he was trying to talk to me. Numbly I watched in awe. *How could this be?* I seemed to be thinking while in a place that was beyond where my mind could go.

I stared at Comanche's feet, wondering why they did not thunder loudly. As he danced and danced, his hooves made not the slightest sound. The dust did not fly when they touched the ground after every full turn. *I must be having a vision.* This thought came to me as wordless talk that formed without thought and seemed to be coming from the front instead of the back of my head.

On a higher level I knew that I was witnessing a miracle. Comanche had never been trained like a Lipizzaner, the magical white horses trained and shown at the Spanish Riding School of Vienna. Although he loved to rear up after a long, fast gallop up any hill, his muscles usually only supported rearing half as high as he did that night. Now, at 1:30 in the morning, in the glimmer of a full moon, he stood totally straight up in the air. Like the feather on an eagle's wing, he flew around and around. I sensed that he was trying to tell me something, to get through to me in my sorrow. I knew instinctively that Spirit was here, doing this with him, lifting him up. Comanche was being held in the arms of unseen angels, visible only through the eyes of my deepest grief.

But then Comanche always had been the strangest horse in our herd. One day, when our mare was waiting to foal at the boarding farm next door, Comanche was all alone in the pasture. I came out to bring him his evening alfalfa flake of hay. As I drove up to the side of the fence, he came galloping full tilt and made a skidding halt. I got out of my truck and waited for him to come to me. He shook his beautiful head, whinnied, turned, and galloped back to the dividing fence in the middle of the pasture. There I saw a strange horse standing in the neighbor's pasture. Comanche stood stock-still in front of that horse, touched his nose to his own leg, then shook his head, turned around, and came flying back to me.

I asked, "What is it, Comanche?"

He whinnied, more like a scream, then turned around and repeated his flying gallop back to the new horse. I climbed under the barbed wire and followed him. Obviously he was telling me to come with him.

What I found horrified me. This new horse's front legs were all entwined in the barbed wire while he bled profusely. Instantly I knew what had happened. Comanche and he had been fighting over the fence in a territorial bickering match. The new gent on the block had struck out with his front legs at Comanche and gotten wrapped up in the barbed wire. It had torn through the skin, right to his bone. Ordinarily horses will keep struggling and fighting the wire until they drop from fatigue. But this one was not moving a muscle.

Comanche's first owner had trained him to stand still when his legs touched anything. He would stop on a dime if the saddle shifted even half an inch. He would still when the rider dropped the reins to the ground, a practice known as ground tying. Now it appeared that Comanche had taken it upon himself to put his face into the other stallion's face and relay the message: *Do not move!* And it had worked.

That horse had not moved a hair. Instead he had waited and waited and waited. It must have been many hours before I found him because he had arrived around midday.

I ran back to my truck, got out the wire cutters, and freed the horse. Meanwhile some people had stopped to watch me. They were commenting, "Watch out. That horse will bolt. He will kick. He's panic-stricken."

I freed the horse's legs, and then he simply turned around and walked off. Then he came back and looked at me, straight in the eye. He lifted up his torn leg and put it in my hands. He bowed his head and held it in front of my face, obviously asking me to aid him. I went back to the truck for some balm and put it on his wounds. His tendons had been torn to bits. It all looked very bad.

Meanwhile Comanche watched intently from behind the downed wire fence. After I finished tending to the horse's wounds, the injured animal thanked me by whinnying softly and putting his head over my shoulder. Comanche followed me closely as I walked to my truck. He kept holding his head next to mine. In utter silence, I could hear his gratitude. He had been his unearthly self, the guardian angel of the neighborhood, and had lived up to the nickname Pegasus that I had given him, after that magical horse with wings of ancient Grecian lore.

This night, when my Pegasus again transformed into a guardian angel and gave me an angelic vision, he had transported me into a state of nothingness, of altered awareness. I had watched my beloved horse dance and float in the light of the full moon. It was a gift that engraved itself onto my soul. Comanche had danced into my being with the message that my husband was not gone. *No, no, no*, he had said as he shook his head over and over again. *Your Beloved is not gone. He is free. He is dancing into Creation itself. Be joyous for him. Dance with him and with me.* But I was gone. I could not hear. I knew I should rejoice — being enlightened about crossing over and knowing that death does not exist. But I was petrified of living without my comforter, the light of my life. I had hit bottom. On this night Comanche had danced in the moonlight to bring me out of my despair.

For twelve more years, I kept Comanche with me, even at times cutting down on my food to pay his board at our friend's ranch. He always smiled when I came to see him. Always carried me bareback around the neighborhood. Always leaned into me as I whispered into his ear, "You are my Pegasus. You know that, don't you?"

When Comanche passed away at age twenty-six, his spirit refused to leave his body. As he lay on the ground, struggling to get up again, I understood that he didn't want to leave me. In my panicked mind, even though I am not Catholic, I called out to the only person

I knew who could help, and that is Mother Mary. "Please, please, please, Mother Mary," I desperately prayed, "make yourself look like me. Put on my grubby little cap, my scruffy shirt, and my faded jeans. Please come and take Comanche by the halter and lead him home."

In my inner vision, as clear as crystal, I saw a figure that looked and dressed like me. *She* took Comanche by the halter and calmly walked him up the road. Home.

Meditation

What comfort has a horse given to you when you were grieving or in trouble? How did the horse's spiritual connection with the Divine ease your burden?

Dear Zeke,

Do horses know something important about the invisible side of life? When my horse passed away, she
seemed so calm. I still miss her.

Sincerely,
Light Seeker

Dear Light Seeker,

Horses know that nothing can ever keep two souls
apart when they love each other. Do you understand?
Nothing. That is why your horse was not afraid. She
never went away. Not really.

When you meet your horse again in this life or
another, she will look as she did on earth, but her
body will shimmer with the light of a thousand
stars. The beacon of her love will help to guide you
home.

Wisely yours,
Zeke

Afterword

*I*n writing this book, we asked the horses to speak to us, to guide us in telling their stories. So often we felt the presence of these gentle, spiritually aware creatures as we wrote of their winsome ways, their tremendous strength, their sanguine attitudes, and their hopes for greater understanding between humans and horses. In our contemplations and dreams, we have met with them, stroked their kind faces, and kissed the third eye, the chakra between their two physical eyes that connects them to spiritual worlds with a golden thread of divine love.

As we took our journeys with horses, we speculated that their stories would appeal both to people who already love horses and to those who are curious and want to know more about them. Then, on the practical side, we wondered if reading about such profound experiences would cause amateurs to buy horses without understanding all the commitment and responsibility that is required.

Would neophytes know that to bring a horse home, they need to meet zoning requirements, have a fenced-in pasture or paddock, a barn with stalls and proper bedding, the money and storage for buying hay and feed, and the stamina (and desensitized noses) to keep the horse's living quarters clean? If they intend to board their horse, will they know what questions to ask and what to look for? Will they have the time, energy, and steady income to arrange for veterinarians, farriers, vitamin supplements, and deworming?

What about the horse's emotional needs? Will they choose the horse carefully for a match with their personality and lifestyle? Will they be alert to whether this horse wants to be with them now? Will they stay a true and steadfast friend for life with regular visits, exercising the horse and giving and receiving his or her love? If their circumstances change, will they be prepared to find an excellent new home for the horse? Will they do all of these things for the twenty, thirty, up to fifty years of a horse's life, long after the horse can be ridden or is of any monetary value?[3]

We sincerely hope that if you have been inspired to bring a horse into your life, you will consider being able to satisfactorily answer all of the questions above. We also suggest, as many responsible horse owners have told us, that you find mentors who are experienced in the ways that you want to treat and train a new horse member of your family. Get involved with others who love horses and carefully secure their welfare.

So let's say horse ownership is not for you but you want a horse presence in your life. What can you do about it?

On a personal level, you can take riding lessons from reputable and patient teachers and courses about horse care, personality, and intelligence.

One of the most rewarding ways to become more horse conscious is to volunteer for one of the many charitable organizations that help people interact with and ride horses or that rescue horses. These organizations exist in just about every area of the country where horses live. If you don't have the wherewithal to physically volunteer, charities are always grateful to receive your donations. Animal organizations that are working to pass legislation to protect horses are eager for your financial and letter-writing support. Politicians who sponsor laws to protect horses will be encouraged by your votes.

Every once in a while, as we worked on this book, we found ourselves stopping to ask the horses: How are we doing so far? They nodded their heads and offered a happy neigh of approval, or so we'd like to believe. *Yes, you have emphasized that we are spiritual beings and we see, hear, and understand much more than we say. Yes, you have asked them to be responsible if they bring us into their lives. Yes, you have done your best to tell our stories honestly. We are big into honesty.*

Now we join with the horse and human storytellers you have met in *Angel Horses* to wave good-bye to all the horses who have graced these pages and the humans who have loved them enough to share their stories. Corny but true — Happy trails to you, until we meet again.

Notes

Introduction

Epigraph: e. e. cummings, *100 Selected Poems by e. e. cummings* (New York: Grove, 1959), 2.

1. Lynn Crespo, PhD, "Wild and Free: The American Mustang," *Southwest Horse Report*, November 1999, 1, 3.

2. Patrick M. Leehey, *What Was the Name of Paul Revere's Horse?* (Boston: Paul Revere Memorial Association, 1997), 5.

3. American Pet Product Manufacturer's Association, "National Pet Owners Survey, 2005–2006," *APPMA Advisor*, May 2005, http://www.appma.org/newsletter/may2005/npos.html.

4. David W. Freeman, "Oklahoma Horse Industry Trends," *Oklahoma Cooperative Extension Services Current Report*, CR-3987 (Stillwater: Oklahoma State University, 2005), http://www.osuextra.com.

5. Tim Harlow, "For Horse Lovers, Expo Is a Bit of a Big Deal," *Minneapolis Star Tribune*, April 28, 2006.

6. Penzance, "What Is Natural Horsemanship?" *Naturally Penzance*, http://www.lightband.com/~santa/natural.html.

Chapter 1: Love and Dreams

Epigraph: Matthew Arnold, *Matthew Arnold* (*Everyman's Poetry Library*) (London: Orion, 1998), 15.

1. Denise Parsons, "Paroled Horse: The Kansas Wild Horse Program Gives Inmates and Mustangs a Second Chance," *Horse Illustrated*, April 2006, 86–92.

2. Claire Albinson, *In Harmony with Your Horse: How to Build a Lasting Relationship* (Guilford, CT: First Lyons Press, 2005), 13.

Chapter 2: Healing and Health

Epigraph: Author unknown, "A Pony's Prayer," quoted in June Cotner, *Animal Blessings: Prayers and Poems Celebrating Our Pets* (New York: HarperSanFrancisco, 2000), 60.

1. Peg Meier, "Nikki's New Life," *Minneapolis Star Tribune*, May 30, 1996.

2. North American Riding for the Handicapped Association, "About NARHA," http://www.narha.org/WhoIsNARHA/About.asp.

3. Kate O'Rourke, "Equine Assisted Therapy: Effect on Horses," *JAVMA*, September 15, 2004, http://www.avma.org/onlnews/javma/sept04/040915o.asp.

4. Compassion in World Farming Trust, "Horses Can Teach Us a Thing or Two," *Animal Sentience*, February 15, 2004, http://www.animalsentience .com/news/2004-02-15.htm.

5. Chris Welsch, "For the Love of Horses," *Minneapolis Star Tribune*, July 6, 2003.

6. Candace Pert, PhD, "The Chemical Communicators," in *Healing and the Mind*, ed. Bill Moyers (New York: Doubleday, 1993), 189.

Chapter 3: Courage and Endurance

Epigraph: Author unknown, Copenhagen's Tombstone Epigraph, quoted in Edna Hoffman Evans, *Famous Horses and Their People*, (Brattleboro, VT: Stephen Greene Press, 1975), 69.

1. Edna Hoffman Evans, *Famous Horses and Their People* (Brattleboro, VT: S. Greene Press, 1975), 67.

   Chapter 4: Spiritual Connection and the Afterlife

Epigraph: The Holy Bible, the New King James Version, published by Gideons International (Nashville: Thomas Nelson, 1985), 546.

1. Karin Winegar, "'The Secret...Was Love': The Inseparable *Beautiful Jim Key* and His Owner Changed the Way We Think of Animals," review of *Beautiful Jim Key* by Mim Eichler Rivas, *Minneapolis Star Tribune*, February 27, 2005.

2. Buddha Dharma Education Association and BuddhaNet, "The Great Horse Knowing-One [Courage]," *Buddhist Tales for Young & Old*, vol. 1, Prince Goodspeaker, http://www.buddhanet.net/e-learning/buddhism/bt1_25.htm.

3. Letitia Savage, "Homemade Bliss: Ten Questions You Should Ask Before Bringing Your Horses Home," *Horse Illustrated*, September 2005, 60–69.

Contributors

Chapter 1: Love and Dreams

KEVIN SCHWADERER, "Emily's Song." Kevin lives in northwest Ohio and is an information technologist. His hobbies include a directorship with Personal Ponies Limited (www.personalponies.org), and he also raises miniature horses and ponies in his spare time.

RENÉE CHAMBERS, "The Artist Is a Horse." Renée, her husband, Robert, and Cholla live on their ranch in northern Nevada. Renée grew up on the Jersey shore and moved out West in 1986, the year Cholla was born. "It's so much fun having a horse who is an artist!" See Cholla's paintings at www.artistisahorse.com.

CAROLINE KANE AGUIAR, "Pajaro, the Horse Who Runs with the Wind." Caroline lives in Ensenada, Baja California, Mexico, with her husband, Raul, and their two teenage children, Ricky and Christine. She enjoys writing, playing the piano, riding her horse, and spending time at their ranch, La Bellota. Email: bajarancho@yahoo.com. Website: www.bajarancho.com.

AMELIA KINKADE, "The New Animal Alchemy." Amelia has been listed in *The 100 Top Psychics in America*. A full-time animal communicator, she is sought by veterinarians, animal rescue organizations, and animal lovers all over the world. She is author of *Straight from the Horse's*

Mouth: How to Talk to Animals and Get Answers and *The Language of Miracles*. She lives and practices in California. Website: www.ameliakinkade.com.

CARMAN COLWELL-BAXTER, "Ladigan's Tears." Carman lives in Otis Orchards, Washington. She enjoys her walks by the Spokane River with her new dog, Sheridan. Her hobby is photography. She likes to visit her grandchildren.

SHARON KAY ROBERTS, "Wee Lass and Promise." Sharon's close relationship with her ponies inspired other stories. Her first book was written in the middle of the night when her ponies would call her from her warm bed to write their story, *Honey, a Pony's Story by Honey* (PublishAmerica, 2004).

JO ANN HOLBROOK, "To Love Full Circle." Jo Ann writes a weekly column, "Heartbeats & Hoofprints," about animals and the people they own, which appears in the *Posey County News* and *The Carmi Times*. From her rural Indiana home, shared with husband, Gil, their horses, and a variety of animals, Jo Ann writes for newspapers and magazines, including *Western Mule*.

JANET L. ROPER, "Thanks to a Special Horse, *I'm* a Real Investment." Janet has long been fascinated by relationships of all kinds. For Janet it's about achieving harmony in the Circle of Life, which affects us all. As an animal communicator in Shorewood, Minnesota, Janet has honed her communication talents to help improve the relationship between animals and their human companions. She receives great joy in helping people better understand their animals' needs and desires.

PAMELA JENKINS, "Take a Bow, Sparky." Pamela is the office manager of her husband's veterinary clinic. She enjoys writing about the loving bond between people and their pets. Pamela's story "Tough Guy" was featured in *Angel Cats: Divine Messengers of Comfort,* and "The Booger Dog" was featured in *Angel Dogs: Divine Messengers of Love.*

LOIS STANFIELD, "Zeke and I: The Perfect Marriage of Dreams and Destinies." Lois is a photographer and digital artist specializing in equine and pet photography. She travels to people's homes, farms, and numerous horse shows throughout the Midwest to photograph people, their horses, and their pets. She lives with her dog, Duffy, and her horse, Zeke, in the Twin Cities area of Minnesota. Her company is Light-Source Images and you can find her at: www.lightsource-images.com.

ZEKE STANFIELD, "Ask Zeke." The perfect horse, gorgeous dressage competitor, best friend of Lois Stanfield, patient model for photographs, most esteemed and wise adviser for Allen and Linda Anderson in helping them write *Angel Horses*, lover of carrots.

Chapter 2: Healing and Health

SHERRIL L. GREEN, DVM, PHD, "The Heart of Whitehorse." Sherril is a veterinarian who lives in Northern California with her family. She met Whitehorse on a cold Canadian winter night fifteen years ago. The memory is still so vivid she had to tell his story. Her story is the grand prize winner of the 2006 Angel Horses Book Contest.

DUANE ISAACSON, "How to Embarrass a Horse." Duane is a grandfather and an aspiring writer and artist, and he gentles horses for Heart of the Redwoods Horse Rescue in Northern California (www.redwoodrescue.org).

ALEXANDRA BEST FLOOD, "Miracles Are Something to Believe In." Alexandra is a sixth-grade student in Sandwich, Massachusetts. She enjoys showing horses, playing soccer, and writing. She is now the proud owner of an Appendix Quarter Horse named Mysterious Art. Alexandra has future plans to become a veterinarian and to own her own farm.

LESLIE ROBINSON, "Big Walter the Mule Led Our Family to Alternative Healing." Leslie lives on a farm in Florida. She enjoys cave diving, riding her mules, and loving all the family animals, including two horses, two mules, four donkeys, one steer, four cats, one dog, one parrot, and a potbellied pig. She plans to join her husband, Ric, an equine massage therapist, in a holistic equine therapy practice in the near future.

STEVE SCHWERTFEGER, "Shetland Pony Shaggy's Healing Journey." Steve works at Harper College in Palatine, Illinois. His two sons, Jim and

Jeff, of whom Steve is very proud, are attending and doing well in college. They still continue, after several years, to find time in their schedules to help the animals. Steve thanks his wife for always remaining calm with him when situations arise calling for him to have to leave at a moment's notice to go help some animal.

SHERYL JORDAN, "Our Angel in a Horse Coat." Sheryl, along with her business partner, Jennifer Freestone, is the owner of a lesson stable and equine therapy program, "Kindred Spirits Horsemanship & Riding Instruction," in western Maryland (www.kindredspiritshorseman ship.com). Her daughter, Angela, is planning on pursuing a career in environmental law because of the appreciation of nature that Sugar gave her. Sugar has a fan club of young ladies, and Sheryl has received more offers, up to $20,000, for his purchase. He is still not for sale. He will always stay a member of the family.

CHRISSY K. McVAY, "Soul-Saver Horse." Chrissy lives in the mountains of western North Carolina with her family. Her writing has been published in *Aim Magazine*, *Wild Violet*, cowboypoetry.com, and many other publications. Her novel, *Souls of the North Wind*, was released in June 2005. More of her writing can be viewed on her website at www.Authorsden.com/chrissykmcvay.

LYNN BASKFIELD, "Listening to Horses." Lynn guides people through rites of passage with storytelling, writing, nature, and horses. It is her joy to help people make a living — and have a life — doing what they love. Lynn has an MA in human development and is a certified life coach. Find out more about her work at www.WisdomHorseCoaching.com.

HOLLY LEIGH, "Smooth As Silk." Holly writes, edits, and gardens when not at the barn. Though Silky retired, Holly continues jumping and beach riding with her new mount, North Atlantic.

Chapter 3: Courage and Endurance

ROBERT (BOB) WAGNER, "Angel for a Day." Robert is a retired minister and social worker living in Neosho, Missouri, with his wife, Anneta, and angel shih tzu, Oscar. He enjoys gardening, stamp collecting, church, and activities with other seniors.

LAURA COOPER, "Horses Can Be Heroes." Laura works in Nebraska's ranch country training horses. She has published inspirational and animal stories and book reviews.

SHEILA ANDERSON, "Horses and Hurricane Wilma." Sheila and her Appaloosas share their Colorado home with their family and several rescue animals who never left. Sheila is an equine artist (paloosedesigns.com). Sundance and Chevy, retired show horses, now enjoy mountain trail rides and carrots.

DAWN NELSON, "The Little Sorrel Mare Who Saved My Life." Dawn was born and raised on, married into, and will most likely die on a cattle ranch, on a horse. She spends most of her free time traveling to shows with her American quarter horses.

FRED WICKERT, "Mule Intelligence." Fred lives with his wife, birds, and animals in Gilboa, New York, in the Catskill Mountains. He takes care of developmentally disabled people in their home.

SUSAN CHERNAK MCELROY, "Fashion." Susan is the author of *Animals as Teachers and Healers*, *Animals as Guides for the Soul*, *Heart in the Wild*, and *All My Relations*. She offers lectures and workshops worldwide, and lives in Idaho. Website: www.susanchernakmcelroy.com.

Chapter 4: Spiritual Connection and the Afterlife

HOLLY WILLIAMS, "A Lovely Freedom." Holly lives with her husband, Willard, on a horse farm in Greenfield, New Hampshire. There they raised their two sons, Tyler and Blake, who grew up riding their ponies and befriending the many children who came to Muzzey Hill Farm for riding lessons. Holly continues to teach riding, flavored with dressage, in which she emphasizes the development of a trusting and respectful partnership between horse and rider and brings to light the realization that we need to listen to our horses more and learn how to read them.

Holly also enjoys hiking, biking, working on her trails in the woods, and all things horse and farm related.

KRIS BOWMAN, "Abby's Secret Life." For thirty-eight years Kris has trained horses and humans to get along better, giving riding lessons and teaching horses to be ridden or driven to a cart or wagon. She lives in central Pennsylvania with her husband, Glenn, five Percheron horses, a Clydesdale mare, two old ponies, one dog, and three cats. Website: www.woodfinncarriagecompany.com. Come for a visit, we'd love to meet you.

MARGARET NORDEEN, "Ginny Goes Home to Her Horses." Margaret has a marriage and family counseling practice in northern California. She lives with her husband, two children, a dog, and four cats. Margaret enjoys writing and hiking and has always been an animal advocate.

SAM YOUNGHANS, "Playing Games with My Pal, Brady." Sam grew up with animals who have shown him love throughout his life. More of his stories can be found at www.parsec-santa.com. He wrote a children's book, *Cancel Christmas*, adapted from a play he wrote that has been produced many times.

FLASH SILVERMOON, "Living with the Mare Goddess, Chinamoon." Flash is an animal communicator and vibrational healer. She's currently completing *Lifetime Companions: Love Never Dies*, her book on animal communication, healing, and reincarnation. Website: www.flashsilvermoon.com.

JANE LARSON WIPF, "Grace." Jane loves being wife, mom, artist, and new grandma. One passion is sharing the story of grief and hope following their son's death. Website: www.sailingonhope.com.

LAURA STEIDL, "Benni Teaches Me to Trust in God." Laura loves being with animals and going horseback riding. She lives in Wisconsin with her husband and two horses. She is interested in learning animal communication skills.

MAUREEN SINISI, "Five Star Winner." Maureen attends a writer's circle, enjoys writing poetry and short stories, and doing aerobics, and is a member of Eckankar. She works as an imaging specialist for a mortgage company.

RENEE VAN ASTEN, "Pegasus in Disguise." Renee was born and raised in the Netherlands and lived there until age fifteen. She has almost circumvented the globe since and ended up living in the States on a horse farm. Since then her husband and all her animal angels have passed away, the last one of which was a full-blooded coyote, who was her guardian angel for seventeen years!

Additional Photographers

Except for the following, the photographs accompanying each story in this book were taken by the contributing authors or Allen and Linda Anderson.

Page xix, 69, 119, 161, 210, and back cover: Photographs of Zeke Stanfield by Lois Stanfield, LightSource Images, Minneapolis, Minnesota, www.light source-images.com, © 2006. Used with permission. All rights reserved

Page 49: Photograph by Jolene R. Bertrand, Avalon Photography, LLC, Edina, Minnesota, www.avalonphotoinfo.com, www.avalonequinephotos.com

Page 101: Photograph by Holly L. Huxford, Oakland, Maryland

Page 131: Photograph by Gary Hoyt, Canton, Georgia

Page 190: Photograph by Diane C. Glassow, Palatka, Florida

Acknowledgments

We give our appreciation to Georgia Hughes, the New World Library editorial director, who has worked on *Angel Horses* with patience and good humor.

We are grateful to copy editor Priscilla Stuckey, art director Mary Ann Casler, type designer Tona Pearce Myers, managing editor Kristen Cashman, our enthusiastic publicity manager Monique Muhlenkamp, marketing director and associate publisher Munro Magruder, the wonderful visionary Marc Allen, and to all the staff at New World Library.

We sincerely appreciate the encouragement from Harold and Joan Klemp, who inspired us on our journey of giving service by writing books about the animal-human spiritual bond.

A special thanks to the contributors who shared their stories about the many cherished experiences with horses. Our deep appreciation to Lois Stanfield and her horse, Zeke Stanfield, for their support and patience. We also greatly appreciate the time that Suzanne Perry and her family spent teaching us about rescued horses.

This book was enriched immeasurably with the stories that people all over the world submitted to our 2006 Angel Horses Story Contest. Thank you to the judges, Marcia Pruett Wilson, Toni Trimble, and Tara Malphus. You helped us select the prizewinners.

We extend our heartfelt gratitude to Stephanie Kip Rostan of Levine-Greenberg Literary Agency, Inc., our dynamic literary agent whose middle name is Encouragement.

Our families instilled a love of animals in us from an early age. We feel a special appreciation for Allen's mother, Bobbie Anderson, and Linda's mother and father, Darrell and Gertrude Jackson. To our son and daughter, Mun Anderson and Susan Anderson, you're the best.

Special thank-you to Darby Davis, editor of *Awareness Magazine,* for publishing our column, Pet Corner, all these years, and to Kathy DeSantis and Sally Rosenthal for writing consistently beautiful book reviews. Lessandra MacHamer, you have always been in our corner, and we love you for it.

And thanks to our animal editors: Taylor, Speedy, Cuddles, and Sunshine. Without you, we wouldn't know what animals think.

About Allen and Linda Anderson

*A*llen and Linda Anderson are inspirational speakers and authors of a series of books about the spiritual relationships between people and animals. In 1998 they cofounded the Angel Animals Network, dedicated to increasing love and respect for all life through the power of story.

In 2004 Allen and Linda Anderson were recipients of a Certificate of Commendation from Governor Tim Pawlenty in recognition of their contributions as authors enhancing the economy and welfare of the state of Minnesota.

Allen Anderson is a writer and photographer. He was profiled in Jackie Waldman's book *The Courage to Give*. Linda Anderson is an award-winning playwright as well as a screenwriter and fiction writer. She is the author of *35 Golden Keys to Who You Are & Why You're Here*. Allen and Linda teach writing at the Loft Literary Center in Minneapolis, where Linda was awarded the Anderson Residency for Outstanding Loft Teachers. They are guest columnists for *Seeing Angels in Animals: A Guided Journal* at beliefnet.com.

The Andersons share their home with two cats and a cockatiel.

They donate a portion of revenue from their projects to animal shelters and animal-welfare organizations.

Please visit Allen and Linda's website, www.angelanimals.net, to send them stories and letters about your experiences with animals. At the website or by email, you may also request a subscription to the free online publication "Angel Animals Story of the Week," and you will receive an emailed inspiring story each week.

Contact Allen and Linda Anderson at:

Angel Animals Network
PO Box 26354
Minneapolis, MN 55426
Websites: www.angelanimals.net
and
www.rescuedsavinganimals.net